West Highland White Terriers

DOMINIQUE DE VITO

West Highland White Terriers

Project Team
Editor: Craig Sernotti
Copy Editor: Stephanie Fornino
Indexer: Elizabeth Walker
Design Concept: Leah Lococo Ltd., Stephanie Krautheim
Design Layout: Mary Ann Kahn

T.F.H. Publications
President/CEO: Glen S. Axelrod
Executive Vice President: Mark E. Johnson
Publisher: Christopher T. Reggio
Production Manager: Kathy Bontz

Discovery Communications, Inc. Book Development Team
Marjorie Kaplan, President and General Manager, Animal Planet Media
Patrick Gates, President, Discovery Commerce
Elizabeth Bakacs, Vice President, Creative and Merchandising
Sue Perez-Jackson, Director, Licensing
Bridget Stoyko, Designer

T.F.H. Publications, Inc.
One TFH Plaza
Third and Union Avenues
Neptune City, NJ 07753

Printed and bound in Indonesia.
09 10 11 12 13   1 3 5 7 9 8 6 4 2

Library of Congress Cataloging-in-Publication Data
De Vito, Dominique.
  West Highland white terriers / Dominique De Vito.
     p. cm. – (Animal Plant pet care library)
  Includes index.
  ISBN 978-0-7938-3705-2 (alk. paper)
  1. West Highland white terrier. I. Title.
  SF429.W4D48 2009
  636.755–dc22
                          2008043724

The Leader in Responsible Animal Care for Over 50 Years!®
www.tfh.com

Table of Contents

Chapter 1

Why I Adore My Westie

It might not be possible to find a more adorable puppy than a West Highland White Terrier ("Westie" for short). With his dark button eyes and nose peering through the puppy fuzz of fur on his face, he is the epitome of cute. But there is something besides mere good looks about him— he has a radiance, a sparkle, an almost piercing personality. He is alert and inquisitive, just asking to be looked at.

I t's funny to think that such a clearly recognizable breed has a rather murky past. One thing is for sure, though. When the Westie did finally come to the attention of the dog fancy, he was an instant hit. He was recognized by the American Kennel Club (AKC) in 1909, and the West Highland White Terrier Club of America (WHWTCA) is celebrating its centennial in 2009. With 100 years of recognition under his belt, his recent past is well documented.

Origins of the Westie

The mention of white dogs who somewhat resemble the Westie aboard the ships of the Spanish Armada would lead one to believe that the breed was established in the 16th century. This is supported by the additional reference to a gift of "white earth dogs" from James I of England to the King of France in the late 1500s. Certainly a dog as beguiling as the Westie would have had many admirers from the very beginning.

A New Breed

The famous painter Sir Edwin Landseer portrayed a Bloodhound and what would appear to be a Westie in his painting *Dignity and Impudence*, which dates to the early 1800s. Interestingly, at that time it was felt that white puppies from litters of Scottish highland dogs (Scottish and Cairn Terriers) were somehow weak and impure, and

so they were typically culled. But when a sportsman named Colonel Edward Donald Malcolm of Poltalloch accidentally shot one of his cherished brown terriers because he mistook him for a hare, he vowed that he would breed and hunt with only light-colored dogs so that the same tragedy would not happen again.

Others came around to light-coated terriers, too. These included a Scotsman named Dr. Flaxman who developed a white-coated strain of Scottish Terriers that was of a lighter build than the typical Scotty. Around the same time, the Duke of Argylle from Roseneath was also hunting with white-coated terriers. The names given to these early specimens included Poltalloch, Roseneath, and the White Scottish Terrier.

Lest it be thought that function was ditched for form in the development of the West Highland

The West Highland White Terrier comes from the United Kingdom.

The Westie may be small, but he is full of energy.

White Terrier, it's important to consider the demands on a Scottish hunting terrier. He was expected to outwit some crafty game—foxes, badgers, otters, and even wildcats. His job was to hunt the game down and stay on the scent, pursuing it even into the ground, from where he would bark out to the hunter to alert to his position. The countryside was craggy, often steep, and usually dark, and so these working dogs needed short legs, narrow chests, and tenacity to spare.

Debut

The Westie came to the public's attention as dog shows became more popular in the United Kingdom. In the late 1800s, all terriers from Scotland were registered and shown as Scottish Terriers. Fanciers of the White Scottish Terrier formed a club at the end of the century but couldn't agree on a name. With a pressing need to unify the club and move on, the name "West Highland White Terrier" was finally agreed upon, and he made his debut at the Crufts dog show in England in 1907.

The breed had an early surge of popularity, with wealthy admirers breeding championship lines. However, the Westie (and many other breeds) nearly became extinct during World War I, as the very keeping of dogs became a luxury. When the war finally ended, breeders had to patch together what was left of the lines and almost start over. This they did with a flourish, and it is said that the period between the World Wars was one of the best for the West Highland White Terrier, who claimed 125 championships between 1920 and 1939.

Westies and Kids

As mentioned so many times in this book, the irresistible appeal of the Westie is undeniable—and if adults feel it, children feel it ten times more. The Westie is such a magnet for children Westie caretakers must ensure that every experience a child has with their her dog is a good one.

A well-socialized Westie will be happy to accept the greetings and attention of children and give it right back. He will be used to little fingers stroking his head and even trying to pick him up. What he will not be used to—or particularly accepting of—is rough treatment. Although you want children to enjoy your Westie, and vice versa, you don't want your Westie to be handled roughly, teased, or otherwise mistreated by a child's inappropriate actions. This is not only cruel, it's dangerous.

It's great if things work out well by themselves, but don't leave anything to chance. Explain to children that there's a certain way to handle your puppy—no exceptions. If you're not sure how your Westie will react when children visit, crate or confine him until the initial excitement of a visit has settled a bit and you can focus on providing a safe environment for everyone. When the children are ready to play with your Westie, give them one of his favorite toys so that he will be more inclined to play and be happy. When handled and played with gently and respectably, your Westie should be fine with kids of all ages. If he's not, make a note to yourself to work with a trainer to socialize him so that he can accept the friendly advances of children. His life will be richer for it!

The Westie Today

Today, the West Highland White Terrier remains a favorite of all who see and know him. He consistently ranks in the top one-third of the breeds registered by the AKC. Let's take a look at the traits that endear him to us.

Physical Characteristics

For a breed to gain recognition and be able to be registered by a national or international kennel club, it must have a written standard (as well as other documentation to support its legitimacy). A breed's standard is a sort of blueprint of perfection for that breed. It's what defines the breed's characteristics and qualities so that anyone can learn what makes a Westie a Westie, for example, and not a breed that's similar to it, like a Cairn or Dandie Dinmont Terrier. Take note, though, that the standard is only an ideal that breeders strive for. If you have a Westie who doesn't meet these standards, that doesn't mean that you have a bad dog—far from it! Your dog is perfect to and for you just the way he is. Perfection is the nearly unobtainable goal of breeders, not casual dog owners.

The breed's standards are written by people in the countries in which they reside, so the American standard for the Westie is slightly different from that of the Australian standard or the Canadian standard. The wording and focus on important attributes may be slightly different from country to country, but all clearly define the breed for its fanciers and those around the world. It's fun to compare the standards

SENIOR DOG TIP

The Senior Westie

Westies are energetic, bright-eyed dogs who retain their enthusiasm well into their later years. You may not even notice that your Westie is aging until he's ten or more years old. If he's getting the things he needs for optimal health (including proper diet and lots of exercise), he should live a long and full life with you.

It's important to recognize signs of aging, though, and to honor them. These include:

- sleeping more
- getting up more slowly
- resistance to or reluctance to go up or down stairs
- increased or decreased appetite or thirst
- disorientation
- sagging of the skin, especially around the eyes

It can be sad to watch your Westie slow down, but his golden years will be some of your best together—by then, you will know each other well. Cherish and enjoy all the years with your Westie!

of different countries, something that's much easier to do now that they can be found online. The following discussion is based on the AKC standard for the West Highland White Terrier.

Size

The Westie's physical characteristics stem from his original purpose, which was to track, find, and unearth his prey—formidable prey, at that. For this he needed a compact, agile body with a deep yet narrow chest and powerful hindquarters, which provide him with good balance and substance. The ideal height is 11 inches (28 cm) tall for males and 10 inches (25 cm) for females.

The Westie's Head

The head is one of the Westie's most outstanding features—and how can it not be, since it showcases that oh-so-sweet face? The breed standard carefully describes every detail of its correct appearance, saying the head should be "shaped to present a round appearance from the front." The eyes are dark brown and convey an almost piercing sharpness and intelligence. The Westie's ears are described as small and "tightly erect." It was important for a Westie to be able to defend himself against his quarry, and to that end, he has a "powerful" muzzle with teeth that are "large for the size of the dog."

Put It all Together

It was very important to early

breeders that this dog could do his job, and the standard goes into great detail about the proper structure of his neck, topline, body, forequarters, hindquarters, coat type, color (only white, of course), and gait. Put all these pieces together, and what's still missing? The temperament of the Westie—his true nature.

Temperament and Behavior

Is a Westie a Westie because he sports a straight, hard, and white coat? Because of his carrot-shaped tail? Because his ears are sharply pointed at the tips? Well, certainly in part. But he comes alive with the description of his temperament, which, like the dog himself, is to the point: "Alert, gay, courageous and self-reliant, but friendly."

There is simply no ignoring a Westie when he is in your company. He does not elicit the same kind of response as, say, a Golden Retriever or a Shetland Sheepdog. He is more standoffish and aloof, always alert to what's happening around him, while at the same time focused on what you're doing. He is a game dog, ready for action, self-possessed and self-assured. Rest a gentle hand on his head, though, and as he turns his attention to you, for a moment you are his whole world. The pricked ears go back, the face and body relax, and his cheerful nature takes over, reassuring you of his devotion.

A Faithful Companion

Westies are staunchly loyal. They take their position in the family seriously, and they will want to be with their owners through thick and thin. Properly socialized and cared for, they get along well with all kinds of people—even toddlers. Where other dogs are concerned, their defenses are slow to drop, and although they may not instigate an argument, neither are they inclined to back down from a challenge. The best antidote to this is frequent supervised exposure with other friendly dogs.

As alert as they are to the comings and goings of the daylight hours, they are more than happy to doze off for long naps in their owners' lap when the sun has gone down—or to share their bed for the night. In fact, for all his tough-guy history, the Westie can be a really cuddly dog, wanting nothing more than to insinuate himself beside you for hugs and kisses.

The Westie has an independent spirit, but if he's loved and properly cared for, he will be incredibly loyal to you and your family.

Chapter 2

The Stuff of Everyday Life

What if you woke up one morning and found yourself in a completely new house? There were clothes there, but they weren't yours. The bed was comfortable, but you had never even seen it, much less been in it before. You didn't know where the bathroom was or whether there was food there or—scariest of all— who else was in the house with you. Are you feeling uncomfortable just reading this?

I magine, then, what it must be like for your new Westie when he suddenly finds himself in your home. Curious and nervous, he will want to explore everything and decide for himself what he likes—or doesn't. Instinctively, he will search for something familiar. You may be the only connection he has between his old life and his new life with you, and that means that you are responsible for minimizing your Westie's stress.

One way to do this is to bring along something from his former home—for example, a towel, toy, or food dish. In time, the item will have less meaning, but for now it could be extremely reassuring. Another way to do this is to try to have everything you will need for your little Westie at the house before you bring him home. The toys or other items won't be familiar to him, but when you show them to him and respond positively, he will get the idea that they're his and he will come to accept, recognize, and seek them.

Basic Supplies

When you think about having a West Highland White Terrier, a noble animal if ever there was one, you may feel that the sky's the limit with all the things he'll need to feel properly pampered. Think again. Remember, a Westie is a dog, and like other dogs, he has basic needs for basic things. Beyond the essentials, you can have all kinds of fun with everything

from bejeweled collars to Scottish plaid raincoats.

To help you stay focused on what you must have when you bring your Westie home, here's a checklist:

- beds
- bowls
- collar
- confinement systems (crate, x-pen, baby gate)
- first-aid kit
- food
- grooming supplies (brush, fine-toothed comb, nail clippers, ear and eye cleansers, a toothbrush, shampoo)

You should have all your Westie's toys, food, and other supplies waiting for him once you bring him home.

- housetraining essentials (enzymatic stain and odor cleaner, training pads)
- identification tag
- leash
- license
- toys
- treats

Beds

You read correctly—your Westie should have more than one bed. In fact, every dog needs more than one bed. A bed for our canine companions is like a chair for us—they should have a comfy resting place in all the rooms in which we spend a lot of time so that they can be there with us (supervised, of course). Place a comfy bed or pad in your Westie's crate; another where you want him to sleep at night (your bedroom works for him); another in the TV room; and possibly one more in a favorite spot in your home. Westies don't need huge beds, and they like to snuggle, so nesting beds or fluffy pillows will work well.

Collar, Leash, and ID Tag

These are certainly must-have items for any dog. Without them, your canine friend will basically be anonymous in a potentially cold, cruel world. Even the most caring rescuer will have a hard time returning your Westie to you if he doesn't have an ID tag or at least a colored or patterned collar as an identifying accessory. And you'll certainly need a leash to walk your Westie.

SENIOR DOG TIP

A New Home for an Older Westie

If you are adopting or rescuing a Westie, keep in mind that the poor fellow may have been through several homes before coming to yours. He will have no idea of what to expect from you, and it will be even more important that his experiences be as positive as possible from the time you acquire him. An older Westie may have received some training, which can be helpful, or he may have been neglected, which may make him reluctant to trust you or others in your family. Approach providing supplies for him the same way you would if you were getting a puppy. Let his start in your home be a fresh one on all fronts.

Choosing a Collar

As you're searching online or in the aisles of your favorite pet shop for the essentials, remember that practical and purposeful rule the day. From his collar to his food bowl, the essentials are things your dog will be wearing and using every day and that you'll be handling quite often. With that in mind, the first collar and leash combo you should own is one that's versatile and comfortable. If your Westie is distracted by the feel or smell of the material—especially if he's a puppy—he may develop a habit of trying to paw at or chew the collar and/or the leash. If the material of the leash is so slick or studded that it is uncomfortable to hold, you will not enjoy taking your dog for walks, and he needs these much more than he needs a fancy leash.

Keep in mind that the collar your baby Westie will wear is going to be smaller than the one he'll wear when he's mature. Before splurging too much on your puppy (which is tempting), think practical for the first collar, and take your time to find a collar that your Westie will grow into. Select something that will be comfortable for your puppy, washable so that you can keep it clean, and durable so that it won't get too chewed up. A basic buckle collar made out of webbed cotton or nylon is ideal. However, practicality isn't an easy assignment, especially with so many collars from which to choose! You could accentuate your Westie's heritage by selecting a Scottish plaid, or you could emphasize the feminine with a dainty floral pattern or the masculine with something decidedly sporty. You could also go classic and choose leather. Regardless of what you like, you have lots of choices.

No matter what type of collar you end up choosing, make sure that you're able to fit two fingers comfortably between your Westie's neck and his collar. This method will help you select

Choose a collar that isn't too small or snug, one that your puppy can grow into.

the best-fitting collar for your dog. The collar's pattern, however, is all you.

Choosing a Leash

Although you can purchase matching collars and leashes, keep in mind that a leash—even more so than a collar—needs to be something that is comfortable for you to use, durable, washable, and all-purpose. These requirements may limit your selection, but purchasing one that's all these things makes you better off in the long run.

The leash should be about 6 feet (2 m) long or slightly longer. It must be long enough so that your Westie has some space to move around but not so much that he is too far away

Going Organic

For the eco-minded, collars and leashes are available that are made from organic and even recycled materials. Organic cotton and hemp collars and leashes have become so popular that they are available in many stores and are easily found online. Those made from recycled materials are a bit harder to come by but are becoming increasingly popular.

from you or tangled in a long line. Although webbed nylon leashes come in many colors, they can be slippery and difficult to hold; webbed cotton is softer and easy to wash. Your Westie may consider a leather leash to be the perfect chew toy.

Retractable leashes are popular with some. They work with a cord that has a snap on one end that you hook to your dog's collar and a mechanism you hold that allows you to let out or bring in the line so that the length is adjustable. Although this allows for some freedom, it's a mechanism that takes some getting used to and it can be dangerous if it becomes tangled in your (or another dog's) legs. The cord can also really sting and even cut if it is pulled tightly against skin (your dog's, another dog's, or even yours!).

Choosing an ID Tag

An identification tag is something your Westie should *always* have on his collar. If he ever becomes

lost or separated from you, the little piece of metal with his name, your address, and your home or cell phone number can make all the difference between reuniting with him and him being lost forever. Don't forget to get an identification tag right away! There are more permanent methods of identifying your Westie, including a tattoo or a microchip (talk to your veterinarian about these options), and these are both reassurances against possible loss. But people who find dogs almost *always* look for an ID tag first.

Crate and Crate Supplies

If you think that you won't need a crate for your little angel, think again. When used correctly, a crate can save you from the agony and expense of coming home to find chewed furniture, accidents in the house, or other potentially dangerous and

An ID tag should always be attached to your dog's collar.

costly trouble your Westie can get into while unsupervised in a room. It's also helpful to have a crate- or carrier-trained Westie when you travel. He's the perfect travel companion as long as he has his crate for the car or airplane—it's his home-within-a-home when you're on the go. There's a full discussion of how to properly use a crate and how to go about crate training your Westie in Chapter 6.

First-Aid Kit

Doesn't it seem like it always rains when you don't have your umbrella? And when you do take your umbrella with you, it doesn't rain? So while it might seem silly to make a first-aid kit for your dog, you'll be glad you made one up if and when you need it. If you go a long time without using it, you'll be grateful. Either way, you win! See Chapter 5 for details on what to include in the kit.

Food, Glorious Food!

There's a whole chapter in this book on feeding your Westie, which you should read carefully. (See Chapter 3.) Food is an absolutely essential item for your dog, and it is also something that can make him very happy. Your job is to provide him with a food he likes that feeds not just his appetite but the particulars of his body. It's what happens once the food is inside your Westie that's truly important, not how

The Expert Knows

All Those Tags

You may not want tons of tags dangling from your Westie's collar, but he should have a couple. One is his license, which you should apply for and obtain from your local municipality. Licensing not only helps your town understand the dynamics of its pet-owning population, but it also assists in assessing any transgressions against your dog or someone else's. The other tag you should have is the one you get when your Westie has received his rabies vaccination. If you don't want them all jangling about on your pup, keep the license and rabies tags filed in a safe place in your home.

appealing the label is or whether the food is hard or soft.

Keep your new Westie on whatever diet his previous caretaker had him on for at least the first month to prevent an upset stomach. Gradually change the food if you want to or if you need to (switching from a puppy food to one for adult maintenance, for example). Once your puppy or dog is on a consistent feeding schedule, you'll be able to assess what his eating habits are like. Your Westie's appetite (or lack of appetite) can tell you a lot about his overall health, so be mindful of it.

Food and Water Bowls

Your Westie should have his very own food bowl, as well as a separate bowl for water. But which bowls are right for your dog? There are so many of these on the market that you may be confused about what type is best. Don't worry! Consider the size and shape of your Westie's mouth, and select a food bowl that's not too deep so that he doesn't have to extend himself to finish his meals. A stainless steel bowl with a rubberized bottom is a great choice, as it is easy to clean and won't slip on the floor. A crockery or glazed pottery bowl is another good choice because these are generally heavy enough that they won't tip over or slip as your puppy or dog eats out of them. There are lots of great designs available in these types of bowls. Their only downfall is that many of them are deep bottomed and don't have sloping sides, so it can be difficult for a dog to eat from some. Plastic dishes may seem like a satisfactory and economical choice, but puppies will often chew them up. Another consideration is the potentially dangerous chemicals like phthalate used to make plastic bowls, which can leach into your dog's food or water and pose a health risk.

Grooming Supplies

The particular look of a well-groomed Westie is something that takes training to perfect, and if that's what you want for your dog, you should find a groomer you like and trust right away. Hopefully you can get a good recommendation from a dog-owning friend or your veterinarian if you don't know one already. That said, you will want to keep your dog looking good between visits, and for that you'll need some essentials: shampoo, the right kind of brush, a fine-

Safe, not Trapped

A crate, x-pen, or baby-gated area in your home, however safe and comfortable for your Westie, should not be a place where you leave him for the day so that he won't get into trouble. Dogs are social animals, and long-term confinement and isolation will literally drive them crazy. Besides needing companionship and mental stimulation, all dogs have physical needs that must be met several times during the day—or for puppies, every few hours. You can't expect to put your dog in a box all day and think that all he'll want to do when you come home is cuddle. He needs you—or someone—to exercise and attend to him several times a day. You will need to line up some form of relief for your Westie, especially if he's still a young puppy. Until he is fully grown, he must relieve himself and eat frequently. Even when grown, a Westie can't be expected to hold it all day—making him do so is inhumane. If you can't provide regular potty breaks, hire a dog walker to come in and tend to your puppy, or find a doggy day care center. Both are increasingly common and relatively easy to find.

toothed comb, ear and eye cleaners, nail clippers, and a toothbrush. Learn more about keeping your dog looking his best in Chapter 4.

Housetraining Must-Haves

West Highland White Terriers are so cute that it is very easy to forgive them. And that can be a good thing when it comes to housetraining. To make your life easier and help keep your sanity while you're working on housetraining, have a ready supply of enzymatic stain and odor remover and training pads. The pads are designed to lure the dog to a spot that smells like one he'd want to use, which he will. The stain and odor remover is for accidents, which will happen. See Chapter 6 for more details on housetraining.

Toys

The Westie's natural hunting instincts are evident when he plays with toys. These dogs go crazy for squeaky toys in the shape of small animals that can be dragged across the floor. They also like toys that they can pounce on and carry around in their mouths, like small tennis balls or fleece toys. You'll soon find out which ones your Westie prefers—shopping for them can be a lot of fun (and an expensive habit!).

Because you'll want to have some new toys at your house as soon as your Westie arrives, think about what would be best in advance. This will depend on the age of your dog. A puppy is better off with a small, soft toy, whereas an older dog may prefer a soft but durable rubber toy that bounces in different directions. Toys that can hold treats can keep your Westie engaged longer than some of the other aforementioned toys.

Leading manufacturers include safety sheets with their chews and toys to help people select appropriate items. Follow their suggestions, and monitor your dog while he's playing. You don't want him to chew off and swallow large pieces of anything, or the squeakers that are inside some toys.

Treats

You and your Westie will both enjoy cookie time. Dogs like treats as much as humans do, and a yummy little tidbit can brighten your Westie's day tremendously. (A discussion of what types of treats are best for your Westie can be found in Chapter 3.) Suffice it to say that while a treat should be a treat, tossing your Westie potato chips, sauce-laden leftovers, or sweets could undo all the time you spend choosing your dog's nutritious food. These kinds of foods can have other nasty side effects, including giving your Westie gas, or worse, diarrhea or indigestion. That's not a treat for anyone!

Stainless steel food and water bowls are easy to clean and virtually indestructible.

Toys and Kids Just Go Together

Choosing toys for your Westie is something your kids will love to do—they enjoy picking out toys for themselves, so why not for their new furry friend? Give them a price range, let them know the qualities you're looking for in appropriate toys for your puppy, and then see what they find. Congratulate them on helping out, and be sure that the one who picked the toys is allowed to introduce them to your Westie.

something nearby. Like a crate, it should not be used for long-term confinement or for penning your pup while you leave the house or yard.

Getting Things Together

Making it easier for your Westie to feel comfortable in your home—his new home—involves more than just having the essential supplies on hand. You should also have them in place. Know where you want to keep his toys; think about where you'll hang his leash after a walk; find an airtight container for his food; and be sure to have several beds for him. (At the very least, put one outside his crate as well as one inside it.) Once your Westie has explored everything and his smell is on his things, they will become more and more familiar to him, and he will feel more and more like your home is also his home. Your TLC is the icing on the cake.

X-Pen

Busy moms of very young children soon learn the value of a playpen—a kind of corral in which they can put their child so that she can't wander off while the parent tends to a task in the same room. Puppy parents can similarly benefit from an x-pen, which is short for "exercise pen." This portable containment system for dogs can be set up inside or outside. With a couple favorite toys, a water bowl, and perhaps an old blanket or towel, your puppy will have a wonderful little room of his own in which to romp about while you do

Nutritious treats make for a healthy and happy dog.

21

Chapter 3

Good Eating

Westies approach meals with their characteristic enthusiasm. They are happy to eat, eager for their food, and will normally look at you afterward as if to say "That's it?" Dogs are opportunistic scavengers, and while we all know some who are fussy, we also know many who will eat and eat and eat. It's up to you, the one who provides food for your Westie, to give him appropriate rations, and most importantly, high-quality food.

Quality Versus Quantity: Nutritional Value

So much has changed about how and what we feed our dogs today—and thank goodness! The pet food recall of 2007 was described by some as a wake-up call more than a recall. Why? Because it is easy to become complacent about what you put on your own plate, much less what you put in your Westie's bowl.

Look for Quality

When confronted with the myriad selections in your grocery store and pet supply store, try to look beyond the packaging and think about nutritional value. Every manufacturer wants you to buy its particular brand, and they throw a lot of things onto their packaging. When it appears that a less expensive food is offering the same as a higher-priced food,

remind yourself that while your wallet may be taking the hit in the store, you'll be spending less on veterinary visits if you offer your Westie a higher-quality food. Why? Because the nutrients in it actually feed your dog as opposed to simply filling him, and if he is fed well, his overall health will reflect that.

Now, the most expensive food is not necessarily the best food. Be a smart shopper, not a price shopper. To do so, you need to understand nutritional value.

The Essential Ingredients

Just as there's a food pyramid for people that gives guidelines about the food that should make up our daily diets for optimal health, so too do dogs need certain things on a daily basis to keep them going. These include proteins, carbohydrates, fats, vitamins, and minerals. The agency that oversees

Your Westie's overall health depends on the type of food you offer him. Choosing a high-quality food is the first step toward a long and happy life with your dog.

Kids and Doggy Mealtimes

Some people think that dogs should be left alone while they're eating so that they can enjoy their food uninterrupted. If you're raising a Westie and either have or want to have children, you should train your dog to accept being fed from anyone at any time—including kids. When he's young, sit on the floor with your puppy and hand-feed him. Encourage your kids to sit with you and share in this task. You don't have to do this for every meal, but once in a while is a great training method.

Kids should also be encouraged to help prepare your Westie's dinner. It's easy to show them how to measure out and prepare the food. They can take over asking your Westie to sit for his dinner and will delight in his response. It is so much better for everyone when your Westie is not territorial around food.

the proportions of these nutrients is the American Association of Food Control Officials (AAFCO); it regulates how "safe, effective, and useful" pet foods are. For those of us who are time challenged, it's at least reassuring to know that the industry is regulating pet foods, but it's also true that dogs are individuals. What may be right for a dog in a laboratory may not be right for your dog.

Be a Label Reader

No matter how pretty a package of dog food may be, it must list the ingredients it contains, and these will reveal the quality of the food in the package. Ingredients are listed in descending order by weight. In other words, the ingredient that makes up the majority of the weight of the product comes first. That should be a meat (protein) source, preferably a pure meat source. Look for ingredients like chicken, lamb, beef, venison, turkey, duck, and so on to be listed first. Dried versions of the meats are "meals" and are often close behind.

After protein sources, look for high-quality carbohydrates—whole grains and vegetables. Also search for ingredients that contribute omega-3 or omega-6 fatty acids, like flax or fish oil. What you don't want to see are a lot of by-products, generic "meat meal," processed grains, animal digest or beet pulp (fillers), and chemical additives and preservatives such as butylated hydroxyanisole (BHA), butylated hydroxytoluene (BHT), or ethoxyquin.

Commercial Food Choices

You have several commercially available options for your dog's food, which include kibble, canned, and semi-moist. Let's explore each type.

25

Good Eating

Kibble (Dry Food)

Kibble—processed food that's shaped into nuggets and cooked at high temperatures—is the original commercial dog food. It's a simple idea: Mix together a blend of liquefied food and nutrients, then bake it at high temperatures until you have instant "cookies" in small, easy-to-eat shapes. Today, kibble continues to be the staple of most dogs' daily diets. It's convenient to feed, has a relatively long shelf life, and is fairly economical. Manufacturers modify kibble so that it's appropriate for different life stages (puppy, adult, or senior), energy levels (working dogs versus sedentary dogs), taste preferences (lamb or chicken or fish), and even health conditions. (Some are supplemented with vitamins to help the joints of aging dogs, or they contain flax to improve skin and coat.) Many dog owners like feeding kibble because its hard texture provides some abrasion in the mouth, helping to reduce plaque buildup.

Although there are many things to like about kibble, it's important to remember that for the food to be convenient and easy to store, it must be cooked at very high temperatures and treated with some kind of preservative. The cooking process depletes the food of many essential nutrients—often the very ones that are being promoted on the packaging. For this reason, and to provide variety and flavor, many people add things to their Westies' kibble— organic chicken broth, steamed vegetables, cooked meats, and even some fruits.

Canned Food (Wet Food)

Dog food that comes in cans is another kind of mixed stew similar to the formula used for kibble, but instead of being baked into small pieces, the water and blood and other juices are left in, and the food is canned and sealed. The smell of canned food drives most dogs crazy, and they typically gobble it all right up.

If dogs like canned food so much and you can find canned food with relatively wholesome ingredients, why not feed it exclusively? Well for one, it's fairly expensive, and because they don't have to chew it, dogs frequently slurp it down and finish their meals much faster. It's also relatively high in fat and calories, especially when compared to kibble. Lastly, it doesn't digest as well as kibble or a harder food, so your Westie may have runny, particularly stinky feces.

A high-quality canned food can be an excellent addition to a kibble-

Dry food, or kibble, is the most popular commercial diet for dogs.

based meal, however. It provides the flavor, texture, and smells that are most appealing to dogs and can be mixed in with kibble to make the whole meal more attractive. Canned food needs to be refrigerated after it's opened to keep it fresh until the can's contents are used up.

Semi-Moist Food

There are fewer and fewer semi-moist foods on the market, and that's good news for dogs because they typically contain or contained many additives to keep them soft, food coloring to make them look like ground meat, and lots of chemicals to keep them fresh and consistent in appearance. Opening a patty wrapped in cellophane and dropping it into your dog's bowl without having to scoop anything out, mix anything in, or otherwise prepare your dog's food was considered the ultimate luxury.

For the long-term health of your Westie, semi-moist foods are best avoided. Many treats are packaged this way now, and people think that by feeding high-quality food, they can indulge their Westie with these dye-laden, scent-infused, bacon- or bone-shaped soft treats. And they wonder why their dogs have digestive problems!

Noncommercial Foods

Unlike commercial foods, which can be purchased at a grocery store, pet store, or big box store, noncommercial foods are those that are not that easily bought or available, although it doesn't mean that they are hard to prepare

SENIOR DOG TIP

Feeding the Senior Westie

An older dog's nutritional needs definitely change, so consult your veterinarian about what your Westie may specifically need as he ages. All of his bodily functions will change over time, including his mobility, vision, hearing, orientation, ability to control his bladder and bowels, and the health of his gums and teeth. Feeling poorly can decrease or inhibit his appetite, especially if it hurts to eat.

It's important to pay close attention to your senior's eating habits. There are supplements that can help slow the aging process and contribute to improved health. Also, use common sense and respect, such as not overindulging your senior with fatty or rich foods and not changing his diet suddenly. If you're lucky, he'll be nuzzling up beside you for his snack of carrots in the late morning for many, many years.

in some cases. Noncommercial foods are appealing because you can better control what your dog is eating. They do take some time to prepare, though.

Before you change over to a noncommercial diet, research the one that interests you thoroughly. Weigh the pros and cons carefully. Find other Westie owners who may have tried one or are currently feeding one, and ask your vet for advice. Gather your facts before going this route. It could be the best investment you ever made for your Westie's health, or it could be completely impractical for you.

Let's explore some of the more common noncommercial diets.

Raw Diet (BARF)

How could someone feed her dog a diet that sounds like a reaction to an upset stomach? Take heart—in this case, "BARF" is an acronym for the Bones and Raw Food diet. It's based on the premise that the best food for dogs is that which is similar to what they would eat in the wild: carcasses that either they or other animals brought down. These carcasses consist of offal (intestines, brains, feet, etc.) and bones, as well as the muscle meat. A BARF diet seeks to mimic this by feeding raw meat supplemented with vegetables, minerals, and sometimes fats. The most commonly fed meats are raw chicken or turkey.

Proponents of the BARF diet say that their dogs are significantly healthier than those fed on commercial diets. They have great skin and coats; less of a doggy smell; far fewer illnesses, especially allergies;

fresher breath; and more energy. However, detractors say that not enough is known about the long-term effects of this kind of diet; that feeding raw meat can introduce illnesses; and that dogs end up missing many of the other necessary nutrients that are accounted for in commercial diets.

If this diet interests you, there are many books on why and how to feed a raw-based diet, and you should study them and talk to your veterinarian to formulate something appropriate for your dog.

Talk to your veterinarian if you want to put your Westie on a noncommercial diet.

Snacks, Treats, Supplements, and Bones

Snacks and Treats

Of course you'll want to spoil your Westie with treats. A treat for him, though, is almost any morsel of food that comes from you. He's not going to love you less for choosing healthy options over dyed and artificially flavored, processed dog treats, no matter how happy the dogs look on the packaging. Some healthy snacks include small pieces of:

- cheese (low fat is best)
- grilled, baked, or steamed meat or fish (no bones, no sauces)
- raw carrots (preferably organic)
- other fruits and vegetables, including broccoli, apples, pears, steamed green beans, cauliflower, and cooked potatoes
- whole grain breads and crackers

There are also many recipes available in books and online for nutritious, homemade dog cookies that you can easily bake yourself from fresh, organic ingredients.

Supplements

As for supplements, healthy foods are always a good choice. Of course, if you're trying to compensate for a health problem, such as slowing down, poor coat, or excessive itching, consult your veterinarian about what's best for your Westie.

Bones

The classic image of a happy dog is one with a giant bone. You may be able to snap such photos of your Westie this way, but proceed with caution. First, never offer cooked bones as these are brittle and can splinter, and the shards can cause internal damage. Offer sterilized beef bones or a frozen marrow bone. Start with small bones, and monitor your dog's chewing to be sure that he doesn't swallow a large piece. Don't give your Westie bones too often; reserve them as special treats.

Home-Cooked Diet

Dogs are scavengers, with millions of years of evolution behind them that have gone into perfecting being around when something edible falls to the ground or otherwise becomes available. It's how they have adapted to the world and why they like to stick around their humans—we are a great source of food that's relatively easy to come by. The premise behind home-cooked meals for dogs is that this is how they survived beside us for centuries. We cooked something, and part of it was left for our dogs. Today, a home-cooked meal is given a lot more attention to ensure that it has all the necessary nutrients, but the same idea still holds true. If you have the time and inclination to do the research and cooking that's required to provide a balanced home-cooked diet for your Westie, consider giving it a try.

Prescription Diets

Pets, like people, suffer from conditions that can be treated with special prescription diets. Your veterinarian will assist you in selecting one if you both agree that your Westie could benefit. These foods can usually be purchased directly from your vet.

When to Feed

If your Westie is a young puppy, he will need to eat several times a day—at least four. As he ages, the number of meals can be cut back to three. By eight months of age, he should be doing fine on two meals a day. For dogs like Westies for whom mealtimes are some of the best of the day, it is unfair to drop down to one large meal a day. Say that he could consume his entire day's ration in 15 minutes or so—what is he to do or look forward to for the rest of the day? He could become obsessed with wanting to find more food as the day wears on. Why torture him or yourself? Indulge your Westie twice a day to make him happy.

Your Westie may scarf down his meals and look at you for more as if he hadn't even eaten. Do not offer seconds or thirds—obesity in dogs can lead to serious health problems.

Figure 3.1
Feeding Chart for an Average Westie

	Puppies (6 weeks–6 months)	Adolescents (6-12 months)	Active Adults (1–6 years)	Sedentary Adults (2–6 years)	Seniors (6+ years)
Times per Day	3–4	2	2	2	2
Amount	¾ cup kibble 1 tbsp. canned	1½ cups kibble 1 tbsp. canned	½ cup kibble 1 tbsp. canned	¼ cup kibble 1 small tbsp. canned	¼ cup kibble 1 dollop canned food
Best Food	Commercial puppy food: 90% kibble, 10% canned	Commercial maintenance food: 90% kibble, 10% canned	Commercial maintenance food: 90% kibble, 10% canned	Commercial maintenance food: 95% kibble, 5% canned	Commercial maintenance food: 90–95% kibble, 5–10% canned

The other thing about feeding a smaller quantity with greater frequency is that it allows you to truly monitor how your Westie feels every day. If he is typically an enthusiastic eater and you come home from work and are met with a disinterested dog, you know immediately that something may be bothering him. When a dog with a healthy appetite suddenly can't eat, something is wrong.

The best times to feed are in the morning—after your Westie has been out to relieve himself—and the late afternoon or early evening, preferably well before you are sitting down to eat your dinner.

How Much to Feed

Whatever you do, don't look to your Westie to tell you whether enough is enough! His answer will always be "More! More! More!" Of course he's adorable. Of course you want to show him how much you love him. So put a leash on and go for a walk, then give him a baby carrot when you come back. It's up to you to monitor your Westie's weight.

It may seem like you have your dog on survival rations, but for the sake of his long-term health, try to stick to the suggestions in Figure 3.1.

Remember that the information in Figure 3.1 is only a guideline. If your Westie seems thin and perpetually

Mealtime can be
training time, too. Food
is the perfect motivator
to get your Westie to
sit and wait.

hungry, increase the amount or
frequency of his meals. If he's getting
chubby, start cutting back slowly and
swapping out some kibble or canned
food for grated carrots, apple pieces,
steamed broccoli, and other healthier
options. More exercise is also very
important for overweight dogs.

Diet and Skin and Coat Concerns

When you see a ring full of perfectly
groomed and conditioned West
Highland White Terriers at a dog
show, you might think that those
angelic-looking dogs come by their
good looks naturally. But it's not
always so. Grooming Westies for dog
shows is an art form in and of itself;
keeping a Westie in a healthy, lustrous
coat can also be an art form. The
truth is that Westies tend to suffer
disproportionately from allergies that

often manifest themselves through
itching, hot spots, and digestive upset
that can deplete the elasticity of the
skin and leave the coat looking blotchy
rather than glossy. Frequent bathing
further strips the skin of protective oils.

Westie owners desperate to help
their pooches have tried all sorts of
medications and dietary changes. As
of the writing of this book, many have
found relief in what the Westie Rescue
of California calls the "Westie Diet." It
is a high-quality, kibble-based diet that
is supplemented with a pure protein
source (cooked fresh meat) and an
assortment of vitamins and oils for a
healthy skin and coat. You can find it at
www.westierescueca.com/diet.htm.

Feeding Don'ts

So far we've shown you what you can feed your Westie, when you should feed him, and how often you should feed him. We've given you the dos— now here are some don'ts.

Free-Feeding

When faced with a puppy or dog who seems particularly fussy or who is a very slow eater, you may feel tempted to leave him a large bowl of kibble beside his water bowl for him to eat at his leisure. This is called free-feeding. While it may seem convenient, it deprives you, your Westie's caretaker, with some critical information. As mentioned earlier, a dog's appetite can tell you a lot about his overall health. If he seems disinterested in food, it's important to know when it starts, how long it lasts, and what else is happening. Fussy puppies and dogs should be fed much smaller amounts and only given a certain amount of time to finish. They will soon figure out that it's "eat or else" at your house.

Unsafe Foods

Dogs can and usually will eat almost anything. They'll get great enjoyment out of leftover bits from your pancake breakfast or your barbeque dinner, but do your best to only give your Westie the healthiest bits. In fact, reserving steamed vegetables or plain grilled meats for your Westie is a great idea, and these can supplement his daily meals in a healthy way (in moderation). However, there are some foods that dogs should never be fed— chocolate, grapes, raisins, macadamia nuts, and raw onions. These can cause serious health problems. Never offer your Westie any of these foods under any circumstances.

Chapter 4

Looking Good

Westies are both very easy dogs to keep looking their best and very difficult dogs to groom properly. It all depends on the kind of look you want and how particular you are about it. If you have show ring aspirations, start studying now with a handler who is experienced in the intricacies of the Westie show clip. Nearly every inch of the dog is expected to look exactly so, which takes years to master.

T hat's probably not you, though. Or maybe it is, or might be. Do you like the look of the meticulously groomed Westie, or do you prefer the scruffier, unkempt look? You may think that you want your Westie to look rumpled but then you go to the groomer and see a trimmed Westie and realize that you've really let your canine companion get a bit too ratty. Just like a person whose hair is allowed to grow out too much, a scruffy Westie can look disheveled rather than cute. You may gravitate from one look to the other over time, too. Your dog won't mind, especially if you or the groomer lavish praise and attention on him while he's being groomed.

The Benefits of Grooming

If you follow the advice in this chapter, you will be able to keep your Westie looking, smelling, and feeling his best while getting to know him better. That is one of the biggest benefits of grooming your Westie—all the time you spend with him will definitely strengthen the bond between the two of you. Done correctly, it's enjoyable for your Westie because it feels good to him to be fussed over. For you, it's a time to actually craft the look you want, as well as a time to get a hands-on sense of your Westie's overall health. By paying close attention to his body while you're grooming him, you'll notice any bumps, cuts, nicks,

Ask a family member to help out if grooming your Westie becomes more than you can handle by yourself.

swellings, or anything unusual that you might not have noticed in passing. Once aware of these things, you can monitor them so that you can take your Westie to the veterinarian if it seems that something serious is developing.

Finding a Groomer

You may find that even with the best of intentions, you can't keep your Westie looking the way you want him to look. Many Westie owners take their dogs to a professional groomer. If this ends up being the route you take with your dog, get recommendations of groomers from other Westie owners. Contact a local club if you don't know other Westie owners in the area, and find out who their members use. Schedule a visit with potential groomers, and bring questions. A reputable groomer will be courteous, friendly, and will answer all of your questions. Once you've selected a groomer, expect to take your Westie in about four to six times a year.

Getting Started

Even if you take your Westie to a groomer, there are things you need to do for him on a regular basis. Five primary areas require your attention:

- coat and skin

- ears

- eyes

- feet

- mouth

You will have to inspect and maintain these parts of your dog in between visits to the groomer. Tending to these areas will be a first line of defense against possible maladies— pests, injuries, etc.

Grooming Supplies

Before you get started, you will need the proper tools to work on your Westie. These include:

- canine nail clippers (the scissors or guillotine type) or an electric nail grinder

- canine shampoo

- canine toothbrush and toothpaste

- cotton balls and swabs

- flea comb, metal with very close tines

- grooming table

- hair dryer

- hand clippers (like a barber would use), with a no. 10-sized blade

- slicker brush

- stripping tool

- styptic powder

- towels

Looking Good

Some of these items are pretty straightforward and require no explanation. Others will be discussed later on in this chapter in their appropriate sections. We'll now look at four supplies that are coat-grooming specific.

Flea Comb

If your Westie seems itchy, use a flea comb to go over the area he can't seem to stop scratching. If the comb turns up any peppery-looking specks, chances are your Westie has fleas. You will need to treat him, your home, and any other areas he frequents.

Grooming Table

Because Westies are small dogs who need regular attention to their appearance, it's best to get them used to being groomed on a table from the time they are puppies. This will make life so much easier for you, as sitting on the floor with your Westie to groom him can become awkward. He will probably squirm more in your lap, and it will be trickier to groom his stomach and toes.

You can purchase a grooming table at a pet supply store. Lightweight yet sturdy, the table can be folded when not in use and comes with a hooked arm on which to attach a leash, as well

Always praise your Westie if he holds still during grooming time.

as a padded surface on which the dog can stand. You can also try to use one of your own tables or the top of your washer/dryer as a grooming table, although this means that you will have to prepare it for your dog and clean the surface when you're done. All you need is a piece of nonskid rubber large enough for your dog to move around on and to catch dead hair and dirt for the surface you choose to groom your dog on. You'll have to hold your Westie's leash because you won't have a place to attach it, but once he gets used to the experience, he may settle into it—and you might not even need a leash. However, always keep the leash within reach.

Slicker Brush

This special brush has small wire bristles that are soft yet firm. It will penetrate the harsh outercoat and reach the undercoat, smoothing both together. Your Westie will appreciate being brushed out every day.

Stripping Tool

Some stripping tools require you to pull out while you pull down, literally pulling the hair out of the dog. However, there is one that goes over a dog's body, separating the outer- and undercoats while simultaneously thinning them with a sharp blade. Opt for the latter of the two.

Brushing Your Westie

Keep your grooming tools in a large container so that they're all together when you need them. Set up the grooming table or area so that you

won't need to move too far away from it to answer the phone or even open the door—you never know.

How to Brush

With your Westie on a leash on the table, begin brushing him with the slicker brush. Start at his head and work back to his tail. This brush will remove dead hairs while stimulating the skin. Be sure to carefully but firmly brush behind your Westie's ears, along his sides, down and around his legs where the coat is more profuse, and over his whole tail.

From his body, move on to his head, where you'll want to pay extra

39

Looking Good

attention. Using cotton balls dampened with tap water, carefully wipe around his eyes and nose to remove any built-up discharge. To sculpt the head a bit between visits to the professional groomer, use the stripping tool to gently dislodge longer hairs.

Bathing Your Westie

Because they are low to the ground and white, Westie owners find that they like to bathe their dogs fairly regularly. Because frequent bathing can dry the skin, it is very important to choose a mild shampoo that's *for dogs only*. Even baby shampoo for humans is not appropriate for dogs. The Westie's coat should be harsh, so you don't have to use a conditioner.

Supplies

One of the most common mistakes people make when bathing their dogs is to forget to gather all their supplies before even thinking about bringing

their dog to the place where he'll get a bath. Also, be sure to put a nonstick plastic mat in the bathing vessel, whether it's your bathtub, a sink, or a designated large plastic container. Without traction, your Westie can become afraid and panicked, which doesn't make for a positive experience.

You'll also need shampoo; cotton balls to protect his inner ears from getting wet; a pitcher for pouring water over him if you don't have a detachable shower head or sink sprayer; and a few towels for drying him off.

How to Bathe

When everything's organized, start running the water. You want warm water—the temperature should be comfortable for both you and your dog. If the water gets too hot, you run the risk of harming your Westie.

Next, place him in the water. Put the cotton balls in his ears to prevent any water from

Grooming From the Inside Out

You could spend hours working on your Westie so that he looks like he could compete at the Westminster Kennel Club show. You could trim his whiskers, bathe him with the finest shampoo, use a shine-enhancing conditioner on his coat, and make sure that every hair was in place. But if your Westie is itching, if his fur feels dry or thin, if there's an odor coming from any part of his body, or if he lacks the charming personality of a Westie, he won't look good for long. On the other hand, if you feed your Westie well, give him plenty of exercise and fresh air, stimulate his mind and his senses, groom him occasionally (and take him to the professional groomer a few times a year), and just delight in his enthusiasm for living, you will have a very healthy dog. Feeling good is a large part of looking good.

going down them. Do not jam them in, but don't allow them to come loose. Remove his collar so that you can wet him all over. Carefully use your tub's spray nozzle to wet him down, or use the pitcher to pour water over his body. Once he's completely wet, turn the water off and apply the shampoo. Don't put it directly on his head—you don't want too many suds around his face, as the shampoo can get into his eyes and sting. Start at the neck and work backward, rubbing the shampoo into a nice lather with your hands. Be sure to get his legs, stomach, and tail, too. To clean his head, take a small amount of lathered shampoo and work it onto the top of his head with your fingertips.

When you've scrubbed him all over, turn the warm water back on and begin to rinse. It is very important that all traces of the shampoo are rinsed off, so be very thorough. This is where having a detachable shower head or sink sprayer helps greatly, as you'll want to get the water on his stomach and between his legs. When rinsing the head, direct the rinse water toward his neck to keep the shampoo from running into his eyes and ears.

Drying

When your Westie is thoroughly rinsed, turn the water off and see if he'll shake himself off in the tub or sink. Whether he does or not, wrap a towel around him and lift him out. Put his collar on so that you can keep him from dashing off (or if you're in the bathroom, close the door to prevent an escape). Allow him to shake, and then start massaging

SENIOR DOG TIP

Grooming Your Older Westie

As your Westie gets on in years, he will become more sensitive to your touch and the feel of brushes, toenail clippers, being bathed, having his teeth brushed—all aspects of grooming. Be considerate of your senior, and be gentle. You'll know each other pretty well by this time, so you'll have a much greater level of trust and understanding. He will appreciate the fact that you keep him looking good, and he will feel better if he is brushed and combed and taken care of.

Older dogs tend to get more gunk around their eyes, and their teeth and gums should be examined more often. They also tend to develop fatty tumors and other lumps. Point them out to your veterinarian at the next examination to be sure that they are nothing serious.

him with the towel to absorb as much water as possible. Dogs typically love this part, so indulge him in a good rub. Use as many towels as you need to get him as dry as possible, then take him to a warm room where he can dry

Looking Good

without getting anything messy—the kitchen is a good spot. Put a baby gate up so that he can't run all over the house, and don't let him out until he's dry. Otherwise, he might go roll in something and you'll have to run another bath and start over.

If you want to dry him with a hair dryer, keep it on low so that you don't frighten him or burn his skin. Most dogs can learn to enjoy this—it fluffs their fur nicely. When he's dry, brush him and then admire how handsome he looks. And by the way, a cookie is always a nice treat after bath time!

Ear Care

Next, clean your Westie's ears. They should appear a healthy shade of pink inside and should not smell. If you notice anything unusual in the ear, take your Westie to the veterinarian for a culture—he could have an ear infection. There are lots of natural-based cleaners for ears out there now. Do your research to find the one that's best for your Westie. (Your vet can recommend good products.)

Eye Care

Wipe the area around your Westie's eyes with a wet cloth whenever you see debris. He may experience what's called "tearstaining," which appears as brownish streaks under the eyes. There are commercial products available that can remove these stains (always apply them carefully), but they don't correct the underlining cause of the staining. Sometimes all that's needed to fix this is a change in diet, but sometimes tearstains may be caused by a problem that only your veterinarian will be able to diagnose and treat.

Nail Care

This is a necessary part of the grooming procedure that many people are uncomfortable doing. The reason is that if you cut too much of the nail, it will not only hurt him but it will also cause him to bleed profusely. This happens when the quick—the blood vessel in the nail—is ruptured. Knowing this, it is hard not to approach trimming the nails with trepidation and fear.

Walking your dog on concrete regularly will help keep his nails filed in between trimming sessions.

An accumulation of tarter on your dog's teeth can lead to erosion of the gums and infection. Brush them regularly to prevent this.

How to Trim the Nails

But fear not! You can train your Westie to be a good boy while his nails are being done, and soon he'll be offering you his paws. To do this, be gentle, stay positive, and start small. Condition your Westie to enjoy having his paws handled by giving him a treat while you reach for and stroke his paws. When he's comfortable with you touching his feet (and happy to be getting treats for it), start holding onto his paws while you give him a treat and tell him what a good boy he is.

When you've done this for a few days—without bringing the nail clippers into sight—begin using the clippers. With your Westie standing on a nonskid surface, hold a treat firmly in one hand while taking one nail into the clipper with the other. Snip only the very tip of the nail off, then let your dog nibble on the treat. Snip, nibble; snip, nibble. Do one paw one day and another the next. If you are having difficulty doing this all by yourself, enlist the help of a family member to either hold the treat or to cut your dog's nails. Work slowly and steadily, and eventually you can make nail trimming part of your regular grooming routine.

What to Do if You Cut the Quick

If you do cut into the quick and the nail starts to bleed, first put a paper towel or tissue (or even better, a gauze pad) on it to catch the blood while you get out and then apply some styptic powder. This is a clotting agent that will stop the bleeding. Always keep some on hand so that it's readily accessible for such an emergency. Also, don't let your dog run around the house with a cut nail, or you'll be cleaning up blood spots for hours. Because it can take a long time for the bleeding to stop, stay with your dog and try to keep him as calm as possible until it does.

Dental Care

There you are, curled up on the couch with your Westie in your lap, watching your favorite show on TV. Your Westie looks up at you lovingly, then starts to pant. You take a whiff of his hot breath and... well, it stinks. Really badly. You're distracted and upset—the moment is ruined.

There are several factors that contribute to the smell of your Westie's breath. One is diet. If you're feeding him a poor-quality food and it's not digesting well, it will percolate out of both ends of your Westie. Yuck! The other factor is how clean you keep his teeth. Imagine what your mouth would smell like if you never brushed, or how it would feel, or what it could mean for your health.

If you don't brush your Westie's teeth, over time the plaque will build up and cause gingivitis, deteriorating the gum line and potentially introducing bacteria into

The Expert Knows

Grooming for Good Health

Besides being a great bonding time, going over your Westie while you groom him is a great way to assess his overall health. Does his coat seem thick and healthy? Are his eyes shiny? Are his gums a healthy shade of pink? Is the area around his tail clean? Can you feel any lumps or bumps? Do you notice any thin patches of fur? Does he whimper and pull away when you touch a certain area of his body?

When you groom your Westie regularly, you will notice when something doesn't look, feel, or smell right. You can keep an eye on any of these things to see if they worsen. If they do, call your veterinarian to have your Westie checked out.

the bloodstream through the gums. Your veterinarian will examine your Westie's mouth when she gives him his checkups, and if she notices significant plaque buildup, she will recommend that your Westie be given a thorough cleaning. However, dogs won't sit still while this is being done to them, so they must be anaesthetized during the procedure, making it quite the undertaking.

How to Brush the Teeth

So for the health of your Westie—and so you will always enjoy being close to your dog—get into the habit of brushing his teeth. Use a toothpaste that's made specifically *for dogs only*—human toothpaste will make your dog sick. Dog toothpaste comes in flavors we would never consider enjoyable (chicken, peanut butter, and others), but dogs love them, and your Westie is no exception. Using your fingertip or a toothbrush made for dogs, work the paste over the teeth and the gum line, reaching back so that the molars are scrubbed, too. Don't worry about doing a perfect job, and if your Westie frets, brush only a little at a time. Because the toothpaste tastes good, your Westie should come to enjoy the experience. Veterinarians would like us to brush our dogs' teeth every day, but a more realistic objective could be at least several times a week.

Chapter 5

Feeling Good

Good health starts from the inside out, and it is certainly something you can influence by making sure that your Westie has a proper diet, gets plenty of exercise, and receives quality overall care. These are preventive measures that are the foundation upon which your Westie can lead a long and happy life. This chapter covers the basics of what you should know to provide good overall care, including how to find the best veterinarian; what to know about the annual exam; what vaccinations your Westie needs (and when); what breed-specific illnesses you need to be aware of; how to handle general illnesses; and what kinds of alternative therapies might help your furry friend.

Finding a Veterinarian

Your choice of veterinarian is really important. Why? Because besides you and your family, it is your veterinarian who will be giving your Westie the best care possible. To do that, the vet you choose has to get to know both you and your dog. Because your Westie can't verbalize his condition, you must speak for your dog—you are the first one to notice if something's bothering him, and therefore you must describe his symptoms. Your vet's advice will depend on what you tell her and what she finds after a thorough examination. If you aren't completely comfortable with the vet who cares for your Westie, you will compromise the care he receives. Like your own family doctor, your Westie's vet should be someone you feel comfortable calling any time with any concerns. When you visit, she should give you her full attention and talk to you about what she's noticing regarding your Westie.

Besides the veterinarian, the facilities and staff should be equally conscientious and responsive. You will be able to tell if the technicians truly care for animals by the way they handle them in the waiting room. What if your Westie needs to stay overnight for observation? Can you be sure that he will be well taken care of in a safe and sanitary environment? These are the kinds of things you need to think about before they become significant issues that interfere with the care your Westie might receive.

If this doesn't sound like the

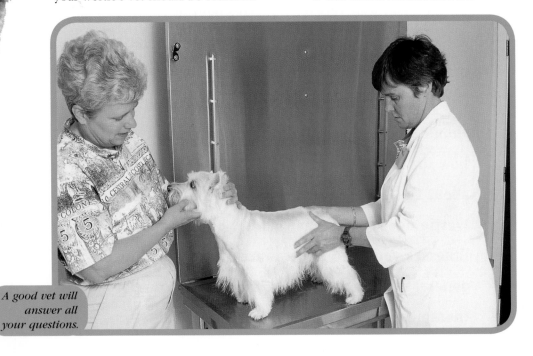

A good vet will answer all your questions.

veterinarian and clinic you currently visit, you may be wondering how you find such a person and place. There is no getting around it: You must visit the clinic, talk to the vet and staff, and trust your instincts. Your Westie's breeder may have a recommendation as well. Because breeders work especially closely with vets, their recommendation is a good starting point. Remember, though, that their opinion is their opinion, and it doesn't mean that you'll be comfortable with their choice. You could do a search through the phone book and make appointments with nearby vets, or you could ask a friend or acquaintance in your area for a recommendation. Start with someone who takes really good care of her dog(s); she will probably be on good terms with her vet. The American Animal Hospital Association

(AAHA) has a list of affiliated veterinarians by city and state on its website, www.aahanet.org.

All this research may seem like a lot of work, but it's worth it for your Westie's health.

The Annual Examination

It's both exciting and potentially nerve-racking to bring in your puppy or dog for his first visit. Everyone loves puppies, and a Westie puppy will certainly steal the show. Everyone will want to pet and visit with him and will make a big fuss over him. Because dogs often fret when they get to the veterinarian's office (it's filled with the smells and sounds of anxious and strange animals), if you're calm and happy to be there, your puppy will sense it and feel better. An initial visit, which will get your puppy started on the road to annual examinations, is critical for his long-term health. Annual checkups are important as well—they can turn up problems you wouldn't know your Westie had.

During an examination, the vet will inspect the following areas:

Eyes, Ears, and Nose

When the veterinarian checks your dog's eyes, ears, and nose, she is looking for unusual discharges or discolorations. She can detect anything unusual by using special instruments that shine light into areas you wouldn't normally be able to examine. For example, contagious illnesses often manifest themselves first through discharge in the eyes and nose. Dull, lifeless eyes can

Feeling Good

be a sign of internal parasites. With an otoscope, the vet can look into your Westie's ears for signs of mites or any discharge or inflammation that could indicate an infection.

Mouth

Oral health is as important for your Westie as it is for you. The veterinarian will examine his teeth and gums for signs of decay or infection. Puppy teeth should be sparkly white, and the gums should be pink and healthy looking. Any swelling, discoloration, soreness, or bad breath is a sign of trouble, and your vet will explain what can be done to remedy them. Another thing of concern is your Westie's bite. It should be level; if it's not, you may have to pay special attention to how his jaw develops as he grows so that he can eat, drink, and breathe properly.

Heart and Lungs

The veterinarian will listen to your Westie's heart and lungs with a stethoscope. If she detects congestion, your Westie may have anything from kennel cough to heartworm. Any abnormal breathing patterns need to be assessed and monitored. As for your Westie's heartbeat, it should be strong and regular. If it isn't, you need to know what you're dealing with as soon as possible, which is why regular visits to the vet are so important.

Skin and Coat

A Westie's fur is naturally somewhat harsh (described as "hard" in the breed standard). He is a double-coated breed, which means that there is a downy layer under the harsher outercoat. His fur is what protects him from the elements and is also what people love to touch when they pet him. Healthy skin and coat are indications that your Westie is healthy overall. A dull or thin coat may indicate that your dog is deprived of some necessary nutrients. Problems usually surface through itching or redness. Things you may not notice yourself can be uncovered by a careful veterinary examination, which can reveal ticks, fleas, or other external parasites. Any hot spots, raw areas from itching, or other oddities should be addressed immediately. Your vet

The vet will give your Westie a thorough going-over at his annual exam.

may recommend some supplements to your Westie's diet to help combat dry, itchy skin.

Abdomen, Back, and Tail
When the vet runs her hands over the rest of your Westie's body, she is feeling for anything unusual in the area of your Westie's stomach and other internal organs, as well as the spine and skeleton. By pressing in certain spots, she can detect any signs of pain or even mild discomfort—indications of more serious problems. It's important to check the area around your Westie's anus and genitals for any swelling or discoloration, too, which your vet will do.

Finally, the Feet
Your Westie spends a lot of time on his feet (paws), so they need to be healthy, too. They should be firm and free of any abrasions or swellings, and he should have smooth skin between his toes. Toenails must be kept trimmed so that the toes and feet don't splay, which can be painful and dangerous. If you're having trouble trimming your Westie's nails, ask your vet to show you how to do it.

All About Vaccinations
One reason that veterinarians put dogs on a schedule of annual visits is so that they can update their shots, or vaccines. For many years, a combination vaccine meant to protect your dog against a host of infectious diseases was routinely given every year. Times have changed, though. The veterinary community is actively reexamining its

Questions and Recommendations
As your vet examines your Westie, she can advise you on things to think about and look for based on what she is seeing and feeling. If you have any questions for her, bring them up. You should leave an annual exam feeling like you've learned more about your Westie and how to better care for him.

approach to annual booster shots, and some questions have been raised. Are combination shots the best way to go? Do they need to be given every year like clockwork? Discuss these issues with your veterinarian, who will have a strong opinion on the matter.

Because you are the first line of defense for your dog, you must learn as much as you can about the pros and cons of the vaccine controversy so that you can discuss it with your veterinarian. Even doctors are wrong sometimes, or they can be overcautious.

What everyone agrees on is that it's essential to give a puppy all his shots, and the combination vaccine available today is recommended. Called the DHLPP shot, it protects against distemper, hepatitis, leptospirosis, parvovirus, and parainfluenza.

- **Distemper** is the number-one killer of unvaccinated dogs. This virus attacks the nervous system, and if left untreated, can cause permanent damage to the brain or central nervous system.

- **Hepatitis** is a virus that attacks the liver and kidneys, causing acute diarrhea that eventually leads to death. It is highly contagious and cannot be cured.

- **Leptospirosis** also damages the liver and kidneys, but it's caused by a spirochete (bacterium) transmitted in the urine of infected dogs or vermin (like rats). Although leptospirosis can be treated, infected dogs will suffer greatly until the spirochete is killed off. Even if they live, they can remain a carrier of the disease, and many pass it along to other dogs.

- **Parvovirus** surfaced as a "new" disease in the early 1980s, and because the vaccine didn't yet exist, many puppies were lost to it. A virus that infects puppies and young dogs, it is extremely virulent and can leave an otherwise healthy puppy dead in a day.

- **Parainfluenza** is a highly contagious disease that's part virus and part bacteria; it attacks the lungs, resulting in a hacking cough.

Other diseases that veterinarians vaccinate against include:

- **Coronavirus**, which is similar to parvovirus.

- **Bordetella**, also known as kennel cough because it is spread where many strange dogs come together, like kennels, dog parks, and dog shows.

- **Lyme disease**, which is caused by bacteria spread through infected tick bites.

- **Rabies**, a potentially fatal and highly contagious virus that's transmitted through the saliva of an infected animal and can be transmitted to

Discuss any concerns you may have about vaccinations with your vet.

If a dog is feeling ill, he will naturally try to hide his symptoms. It's up to you to learn how your dog acts when he's healthy so that you can recognize when something is wrong.

humans. Rabies is the only vaccine required by law in order to protect your dog, your family, and the community.

Vaccinating Past Puppyhood

In the not-too-distant past—and even now—veterinarians have used the annual examination as a time to update a dog on his shots, which meant giving them all again whether a dog needed them or not. Vets are wising up to the fact that all these shots may not be necessary and in fact may contribute to diminished rather than improved health. So today, many give blood tests to assess the amount of a vaccine (or other substance) still in the dog's blood. These tests, called titers, are routine and fairly accurate, and they can alert your veterinarian to whether your Westie may still have enough protection in his

system. For example, if you don't keep your Westie in a kennel with lots of other dogs, he may not need a shot for bordetella—although if you send him to a doggy day care center or plan to kennel him while you're on vacation, those facilities may require it.

Westie-Specific Illnesses

Of course you love your dog and will do whatever is necessary to keep him healthy and safe. Knowing what may be afflicting him is better than being surprised by it later. The first thing to do is ask your Westie's breeder or the person from whom you obtain your dog if she knows of any existing health problems. A reputable breeder will be aware of health problems specific to Westies and will give you information on the testing that's been done with her breeding stock to prevent these

A reputable breeder will know if her puppies have been genetically predisposed to any serious health problems.

illnesses. Someone in breed rescue is probably also familiar with specific health problems and how to address them.

The West Highland White Terrier Club of America (WHWTCA) is especially proactive about the health of the breed. The club's website has detailed and extremely helpful information on the illnesses that can affect Westies at www.westieclubamerica.com/health/concerns.html.

Here are some of the most common diseases that can affect Westies.

Addison's Disease

This is a disease that has to be diagnosed with a blood test, as it affects the levels of sodium and potassium in the body, which are controlled by the hormone aldosterone. Addison's results from the failure of the adrenal cortex to produce aldosterone, as well as the hormones corticosterone and cortisol. (The adrenal cortex is the outer part of the adrenal gland, which is situated on the kidney.) Young and middle-aged dogs are those most often diagnosed when they show signs, which include anorexia, vomiting, dehydration, depression, and weight loss. Medication to control the levels of potassium and sodium can be given, and regular blood work must be done to monitor levels.

Bladder Cancer

Westies suffer disproportionately from bladder cancer, and it is a disease that is being vigorously studied in the breed.

Spaying or Neutering Your Westie

Spaying or neutering refers to the surgical sterilization of your Westie. Females are spayed and males are neutered. While this may sound cruel, there are many benefits to having this relatively simple procedure done.

Your Westie's breeder should have spoken with you about this, or certainly the rescue group or animal shelter from which you got your puppy or dog. There is a canine overpopulation problem in the United States, and besides there being no need to contribute to it by breeding your Westie, there are also lots of reasons that spaying or neutering will keep your Westie healthier in the long run. Everyone loves their dog, but not everyone should breed them.

A spayed female will be less prone to diseases of her reproductive system, but best of all, she won't be subject to heat cycles. These are messy for you and have the potential to attract every intact male dog in your neighborhood—not pleasant! Another thing you won't ever have to worry about is how your little girl will get through a pregnancy and whelping a litter of puppies. Let that be the concern of a professional dog breeder!

Neutering a male Westie will lower his tendency to be territorial, which translates to less marking and less posturing with other males in particular. You also won't have to worry about diseases of his reproductive system. Best of all, you won't have to worry about whether he'll find a way out of your yard to go courting the neighborhood females.

Also called transitional cell carcinoma (TCC), it is typically diagnosed in dogs over the age of five. The cancer can obstruct the flow of urine from the kidneys to the bladder and/or from the bladder to the outside of the body, and symptoms include little urine or trouble urinating. The Westie Foundation of America (WFA) is actively seeking blood samples from affected dogs, as well as older dogs who have not been diagnosed with cancer so that they can try to determine the genomic mutations associated with the disease. Medication is available to try to fight the cancer.

Copper Toxicosis (CT)

Some Westies are born with a liver that doesn't allow them to completely metabolize copper, resulting in an accumulation of the metal that can lead to cirrhosis of the liver. Dogs can appear perfectly healthy for years as copper accumulates. Weight loss, listlessness, vomiting, and abdominal pain are all symptoms, although CT is much more serious than the upset stomach it can appear to be. A diagnosis must be made through a liver biopsy. The disease can be treated with drugs. Researchers are still trying to determine a definitive mode of inheritance for this disease.

Legge-Calve-Perthes Disease

This disease is seen in many smaller dog breeds, including Westies, and is the result of blood not being able to get to the head of the femoral bone in one or both legs. When this happens, the cells start to die, which causes the bone to change shape and lose its ability to function properly. This leads to an irregular fit in the hip socket and other changes. Legge-Calve-Perthes causes a lot of pain, and affected dogs show lameness or stiffness in the hind leg(s), typically between the ages of 3 and 11 months. Although it has been theorized that trauma can initiate the disease, there is also speculation that it has various causes, from nutrition to genetics. Treatment varies based on the severity of the condition, and if drug use isn't sufficient, a femoral head replacement operation is often advised.

Westie Lung Disease

Idiopathic pulmonary fibrosis, or Westie Lung Disease, occurs when scarring is present in the air sacs and connective tissues of the lungs. This scarring may occur because the alveoli (the primary sites of gas exchange with blood) in the lungs are inflamed. Symptoms include a dry cough, shallow or labored breathing, becoming easily fatigued, and upon inspection, scarring of the lungs. Difficulty breathing can also affect the dog's heart because it has to work harder to compensate due to compromised blood flow. Because so little is known about Westie Lung Disease at this time, once a diagnosis of scarring is made—typically when the dog is older—there is not much that can be done to reverse the disease.

White Shakers Syndrome (WSS)

Dogs afflicted with White Shakers Syndrome shake and have seemingly uncontrollable tremors throughout their whole body. Young dogs (nine months to three years old) are most

SENIOR DOG TIP

Your Senior Westie's Health

The West Highland White Terrier Club of America (WHWTCA) has detailed information on problems that can crop up with advanced age on its website at www.westieclubamerica.com/health/aging.html. It is a valuable resource, gleaned from people with lots of experience in caring for older Westies. Knowing what to look for, recognizing symptoms, and trusting your instincts will all help tremendously when it comes to your senior friend.

frequently affected. Handling, stress, or excitement can trigger the tremors, which tend to last all day and can also extend at times to head tilting, weakness of the limbs, or seizures. It is speculated that the cause is an inflammation of the central nervous system, but its cause is still not known at this time. The word "white" was added to the disease's name because it was most often seen in small white dogs. Because it can lead to loss of appetite, dogs with WSS need to be hand- or bottle-fed and encouraged

Feeling Good

to continue eating. Quiet and semi-isolation can help. Medications for the disease can include anti-anxiety and/or anti-inflammatory drugs. The condition needs to be monitored and treated by a veterinarian. Early detection and diagnosis are essential to recovery, so if you notice something wrong with your Westie, bring him to the vet immediately.

General Health Concerns

You will want to be on the lookout for certain things in between routine veterinary visits. Infestation by internal or external parasites are especially of concern, as the Westie is a dog who thrives in the great outdoors (bringing him outside is one of the best things you can do for his mental health).

External Parasites

External parasites are potentially dangerous organisms, including fleas, ticks, ringworm, and mites, that attack your Westie from the outside-in. An attack by any of them is bad news—not only for your poor Westie but also for you, your family, and your home.

Fleas

These pervasive bugs can survive in your home for a long time, so even when you think you've gotten rid of them on your dog, they can still be lurking in your carpet or other corners of your home. Because they reproduce so rapidly, by the time you see a flea on your dog, there are already plenty of eggs in your home. These eggs can lay dormant for a long time under normal circumstances.

Getting rid of fleas and keeping your dog (and home) flea-free is a big business. There are all kinds of products on the market that are designed to help. Depending on where you live, you may need to tend to the problem all year or seasonally. Ask your veterinarian which preventive

If you notice that your Westie is itching to excess, he might have fleas.

FAMILY-FRIENDLY TIP

Kids, Dogs, and Ticks

From the time they're young, we safeguard our kids from picking up ticks when they're outside by applying repellent, having them wear white socks that go over their pants, and so on. Most kids are alert to the threat of ticks and grossed out by seeing the bloodsuckers on their persons. Because they're already thinking about how to keep ticks at bay when outside, it's easy to get kids into the habit of doing the same for their Westie. If they want to help apply a preventive to your Westie's skin and coat, be sure to read the directions and any precautions first.

Fleas tend to gravitate toward a dog's head, neck, groin, and tail, so always check those areas thoroughly when grooming your Westie or after coming in from a walk. If you see any black specks, go over your dog with a flea comb. Crush any fleas the comb isolates with your fingernail, or dip the comb in a jar of rubbing alcohol to kill them. To prevent a problem in the house, change your vacuum cleaner bags frequently during flea season, and pay close attention to your dog's sleeping areas. If you notice fleas in your home, you will have to use a fog treatment to stop the infestation.

Mites

Just when you thought this topic couldn't get yuckier, we come to mites. There are actually two forms of them: ear mites and mange mites. Mites burrow into the skin, irritating the tissue. If your Westie is scratching at or shaking his head frequently, he may have ear mites. Your veterinarian will be able to determine this quickly and easily. Mange mites, on the other hand, infect the skin itself—any part of the skin—and are present as either demodectic mange or sarcoptic mange. Hair loss, itching, and an overall "moth-eaten" appearance are signs of demodectic mange, which tends to manifest when a dog's immune system is compromised. A proper diet is something easy you can do to keep these bugs at bay. Sarcoptic mange causes intense itching that results in red, raw patches or bumps. As the dog continues to scratch the patches—

treatment methods she thinks are best for your Westie—from those that work from the inside-out to those that kill or repel fleas from the outside.

Treatments can have side effects, so research the chemicals you're putting on your Westie and decide whether they're worth it in the long run. Medical studies have shown that animals with compromised immune systems are more susceptible to fleas and other bugs, so keeping your Westie healthy is a good line of defense. Keep a flea comb handy, too.

Feeling Good

which he is driven to do—they become crusty or oozy. Aggressive and immediate treatment is necessary, as intense scratching can become a habit even when the source is removed.

Ringworm

Although not technically a worm (it's actually a fungus), ringworm is a highly contagious external parasite. Infected people and dogs spread the disease when spores drop from their hair or skin. Feeding on dead skin and hair cells, ringworm creates an itchy, scaly bald patch. Ringworm can be treated with a specialized topical ointment but is tough to eliminate because it's a hardy parasite. During treatment, fastidious attention to the hygiene of the dog's environment is critical.

Ticks

There are several species of the vile parasites we know as ticks, and all are bad for dogs. Most common are the brown dog tick (also known as the wood tick) and the deer tick. The brown dog/wood tick is the one that's typically the size of a small bead. It is flat and brown and sometimes has a white horseshoe-shaped line on it. Male and female wood ticks are small and brown when not engorged with blood; when they are full of blood, the female turns gray and can get to the size of a pencil's eraser. Dog ticks can carry Rocky

Mountain spotted fever, tularemia, encephalitis, and possibly Lyme disease. The deer tick is tiny—the size of a fleck of pepper when not engorged. Difficult to see and find when close to the skin, the deer tick is the primary host for Lyme disease. For more on how to identify these parasites, go to www.tickinfo.com.

There are many tick preventives on the market. Discuss their pros and cons with your veterinarian. Depending on where you live, you are bound to find ticks on your Westie (or yourself) at some time, so knowing what to do about them is important. Doctors recommend carefully removing them with tweezers so that you don't puncture them in between your fingers. Grab the tick by the head as close to the skin as possible so that you can

Heartworm is a serious matter for dogs. Your furry friend should be given a monthly preventive for it.

test taken to see if your dog is infected with a tick-borne disease. The sooner treatment begins, the better.

Internal Parasites

The word "parasite" is enough to give anyone pause, but it's even scarier to know that internal parasites are really worms. There are several kinds of worms that can enter your Westie's system through his skin or something he eats or drinks. Even imagining worms growing inside your Westie is creepy; what they really do is downright dangerous. Parasites complete part of their life cycle by feeding on nutrients inside your dog. Fortunately, routine preventive care is simple and cost effective, and it works. By learning what to look for and do, you should never have to worry about worms.

Heartworm

Like the name implies, this is a parasite that grows in the vessels of the heart. If untreated, heartworms can eventually cause blockages and lead to heart failure and death. Heartworms make their way into a dog through the bites of infected mosquitoes. Once the larvae are inside your dog, it can take several months for them to find their way to the heart and start growing. Suspect an infection if you notice a chronic cough, weight loss, and fatigue.

Treatment for heartworm is painful and not always completely effective, which is why veterinarians practically

remove as much of the tick as cleanly as possible. Once removed, put the tick into a jar of rubbing alcohol, which will kill it. When it is dead, you can flush the contents of the jar down the toilet. If you notice a dark spot in the wound, the tick's head is still attached to your dog. You must then contact your veterinarian for further instructions.

You'll need to disinfect the bite spot on your dog. After removing the tick, clean the spot with hydrogen peroxide, then add a dab of antibiotic ointment. Keep an eye on the spot, and if you notice any redness or swelling, make an appointment with your vet. The spot should be looked at and a blood

A First-Aid Kit

This is one of those things that you think you aren't going to need, but when something happens, it's the first thing you want to have handy. Be prepared and put one together in a box labeled "FIRST AID" with your Westie's name on it. Keep the supplies fresh and stocked. Like carrying an umbrella when rain threatens, hopefully if you have it, you won't need it. Include the following items:

- adhesive tape (1 to 2 inches [2 to 5 cm] wide)
- antibiotic ointment
- buffered, enteric, or children's aspirin (not ibuprofen or acetaminophen)
- cotton balls
- disposable latex gloves (several pairs)
- gauze pads and rolls
- hydrogen peroxide 3% solution
- pair of old stockings (for making a temporary muzzle)
- phone numbers of your veterinarian, a poison control center, and the emergency animal hospital (along with directions)
- rectal thermometer
- rubbing alcohol
- small, sharp scissors
- tweezers

insist that you put your Westie on a routine heartworm preventive. The first step is to have a blood test to be sure that he isn't already infected. Preventive heartworm medication comes in the form of a tasty, chewable tablet typically given once a month. It's worth it!

Hookworm

Your Westie can become infected with hookworms if he spends any time standing or playing in an unsanitary environment, such as a kennel that's never cleaned, a dirty dog park, etc. Hookworms enter a dog's system through his feet. They are small worms that attach to a dog's intestinal lining, where they suck blood, causing infected dogs to become anemic and have pale gums. An infected dog's stool may also be bloody or resemble tar. Once diagnosed, treatment is relatively simple and effective.

Roundworm

Roundworms are actually long and thin, not round at all. The width of a pencil when full grown, they can grow up to 6 inches (15 cm) long. Because they multiply quickly, they can cause sudden death if left untreated, particularly in puppies. Interestingly, they can be present in newborn puppies whether their mother was dewormed or not. Because of this, a routine puppy dewormer is necessary. Roundworms can infect humans as well, so attention is critical. Signs of an infection can be a dull coat, pot-bellied appearance, and overly sweet breath with possible diarrhea, coughing, and vomiting. Any

Taking Your Westie's Temperature

If your Westie seems lethargic or out of sorts, and certainly if he misses a meal, you should take his temperature. A dog's normal rectal temperature is 100.5° to 102.5°F (38° to 39°C). To take his temperature, ask someone to help you. You'll need someone to hold him still so you can insert the thermometer—he won't be too happy about the process.

Shake down a rectal thermometer or restart it so that there is no reading. Apply some petroleum jelly to the part that is to be inserted so that it goes in easier. You may want to tie a string around the thermometer before you start so that if your Westie squirms or sits and the thermometer goes all the way in, you'll be able to easily remove it. Once the thermometer is in, wait for either the beeping that indicates the temperature level is reached, or give a mercury-based thermometer about two minutes. Then remove the thermometer and take note of the temperature. Report anything abnormal to your veterinarian immediately.

or all of these signs warrant a trip to the veterinarian, who will prescribe medicine immediately.

Tapeworm

The tapeworm is a segmented parasite that feeds in the host's intestine. Tapeworms are typically transmitted through fleas and contact with dead animals, so keeping your Westie's environment flea-free is a must. Tapeworms feed in a dog's intestine. You'll know that your dog has a tapeworm if you see small rice-like segments around his anus or in his stool. Tapeworms are the least harmful of the internal parasites, but you still want to get rid of them as soon as possible.

Whipworm

The whipworm is the most prevalent parasite in dogs in North America. This is partly because they are hardy and can survive for up to five years in most environments. They are also transmitted through the feces of infected animals, so any Westie who has the tendency to eat feces can potentially become infected. Whipworms feed in the lower intestine, and they can live for months without affecting your dog. Anemia is possible, but for the most part, your Westie will appear normal. Your veterinarian will make a diagnosis by examining a stool sample. Treatment involves both medication and diligence so that the infestation doesn't reoccur.

Keep calm in an emergency— your Westie is counting on you.

Check your Westie regularly for any scratches, insect hitchhikers, or other possible health problems after you bring him in from outside.

Other Problems

Accidents

Accidents run the gamut from a small scratch to a bee sting to a burn or deep cut. If they're not severe, skin abrasions can be treated with antibiotic ointment and bandaging; a veterinarian should tend to burns because they can be extremely sensitive. Insect stings can be soothed by applying a compress of baking-soda paste to the affected area. If your Westie is in pain from the accident (or in general), you can give him buffered or children's aspirin (no ibuprofen or acetaminophen)—just be sure to check with your veterinarian first. Monitor localized pain for its severity, and if you have any concerns or doubts, call your vet.

Allergies

So many things can set off an allergic reaction in a dog—everything from the saliva in a flea bite to something in your Westie's food to a chemical in your carpet. Your vet can perform a series of tests to try to identify the culprit. Once identified, you need to do all you can to remove it from your dog's environment. Without testing for the allergen, though, you can spend a lot of time and effort trying to rule potential culprits out. Get a veterinary diagnosis as soon as possible if you truly suspect an allergy.

Diarrhea

Westies, like people, occasionally experience diarrhea. This can be caused by many things, from a piece of bad food to heat stress to nerves.

You can give your Westie an antidiarrhea medication formulated for dogs to ease the symptoms. (Check with your vet first before giving any over-the-counter medicines to your dog.) Feeding a bland diet of boiled or baked chicken and steamed rice, along with plenty of water, is also a good idea for a couple days. If he doesn't recover fairly quickly, take him to the vet.

Ear Infections

With their small pricked ears, Westies aren't really prone to ear infections because air can get into them and keep them dry. Still, though, because the breed is close to the ground and its ears are exposed to a lot of dirt and debris, they do get dirty. Cleaning the ears should be part of your Westie's grooming routine as described in Chapter 4. Signs of trouble include a foul smell, unusual discharge, swelling, or redness, all of which warrant an appointment to have the ears examined by your veterinarian.

Poisoning

If for any reason you think that your Westie has been poisoned, *call your veterinarian immediately*. Make an appointment to bring him in as soon as possible. While you're on the phone, try to identify the source of the potential poisoning so that you can bring a label or something to show the vet. If it is after hours, call a poison control hotline. The Animal Poison Control Center is run by the American Society for the Prevention of Cruelty to Animals (ASPCA) and has been serving pet owners for several decades—it can be reached at 1-888-426-4435. You can learn more through

Exploring Alternative Therapies

The market for alternative therapies for pets is burgeoning, and getting good advice and making good contacts are critical. A great reference is Dr. Bob and Susan Goldsteins' book, *The Goldsteins' Wellness & Longevity Program for Dogs & Cats* (T.F.H. Publications, 2005). Dr. Bob—Robert S. Goldstein, VMD—has been a holistic veterinarian for more than 30 years; combined, the Goldsteins have nearly a half-century of hands-on experience. The book explores diet; nutritional supplements; vaccination issues; and a full range of natural healing modalities, including acupuncture, aromatherapy, chiropractic treatment, flower essences, glandular therapy, hair analysis, herbal medicine, homeopathy, homotoxicity, music therapy, nutritional blood testing, Telling TTouch, and traditional Chinese medicine. The Product and Services Guide, References, and Resources in the back of the book are invaluable to expand upon a new or already existing knowledge of or interest in alternatives.

the ASPCA's website at www.aspca.org; click on "Animal Poison Control."

Vomiting

All sorts of things can trigger your dog to vomit, from something serious to something minor. Dogs like to eat grass, and they often vomit afterward. Playing hard after a meal may cause your Westie to vomit as well. Infrequent or cause-specific vomiting is nothing to worry about, although you should keep an eye on your dog to make sure that it doesn't get worse. Persistent or violent vomiting, however, is cause to bring your Westie to his vet for immediate attention.

Alternative Therapies

Sometimes called holistic medicine or complementary medicine, alternative treatments are many and varied. In essence, though, the concept is that disease can be treated not just by introducing something that will kill or mask the symptoms of the illness but by exploring its actual root. For example, although there are numerous ways to kill or treat parasites, there are also ways to prevent them from being a problem for your dog (and you) by boosting the immune system, keeping the environment clean, and striving for overall robust health. Dogs can now benefit from therapies as diverse as acupuncture, chiropractic treatments, reiki, herbal therapy, homeopathy,

aromatherapy, and even animal communication. Alternative therapies are worth considering because they can truly make a difference, especially if you're suddenly faced with a condition like arthritis or cancer, where acupuncture or diet could add quality time to your dog's life. There are lots of books on this topic and on the particular therapies themselves that you can explore further.

Chapter 6

Being Good

The West Highland White Terrier wants and needs a fair, firm, positive leader. If you embody these things, training will be infinitely easier. But what do they mean relative to your dog?

Establish Rules and Stick to Them

To a Westie, who is very smart and has a real independent streak, being fair means being respectful. Rules are great, and like children, Westies thrive on them. But rules need to be reasonable, they need to be enforceable, and they need to be consistently applied. If you don't want your Westie on the sofa in the living room, he will need to be taught that it is off-limits. That doesn't mean that he can't enjoy the comfort of the sofa in the TV room. Confused? That's where firm comes in. Allowing him to sit with you on the sofa in the TV room is a fair rule—it's a more relaxed environment, and you can enjoy his company there, whereas if you're entertaining guests in the living room, you don't want your Westie to hop up and nibble on the guests' snacks. Teaching him the difference will require firm training; in other words don't give in! On the other hand, remember that you'll get farther with your Westie when you use motivational training methods. Be upbeat when you're teaching your furry friend, and stay positive for best results.

Find a Trainer

It's easy to read a book and think about how much sense the advice makes. It's a completely different thing to be faced with a problem you've never experienced before and wonder how to deal with it—especially if the problem is a puppy or dog with whom you are madly in love with and don't want to upset in any way, shape, or form. Heed the following advice: Get yourself and your Westie to a professional trainer, pronto! Dog trainers understand that love is blind and that puppies and dogs will develop bad habits if their love-struck owners can't provide fair and firm rules when necessary.

An obedience class will expose you to other dog owners who are going through what you're going through—wondering how to do what's best for their dog and their family. A professional will help you learn how your dog thinks so that you can use language he understands. Attending obedience classes will be one of the best things you can do with your Westie.

A trained dog is just more pleasant to be around. Work with your dog to teach him how you want him to behave.

Finding the Right Trainer

An obedience class can be your ticket to the best relationship you've ever had with a dog. Or like going to a bad doctor, it can disappoint and frustrate you so much that you will be even more confused. It's so important to find the right trainer! Try to get references from a reliable source such as your veterinarian or other dog owners in your neighborhood. You can contact the Association of Pet Dog Trainers (APDT), a national group that certifies its trainers and encourages the use of positive training methods, at 1-800-PET-DOGS or www.apdt.com, to find members who are trainers in your area.

Socialize From Day One

Hopefully your Westie puppy or dog is already a well-adjusted and confident fellow. He became that way by having positive interactions with all different kinds of people and animals in all different places and environments. Because you want him to be able to feel comfortable meeting and interacting with all kinds of people and animals, it is critical to socialize him early and often. Positive experiences will definitely boost his self-confidence, reducing his fear. When he is startled by something, you'll be there to help him make sense of it.

Positive Socialization

When the goal is positive experiences, you must take an active role in setting the stage for your puppy. Walk over to your nice neighbor's house—the family with the kids who love animals and know how to behave around them— and bring along some tasty treats. When you get there, give the treats to the family so that, as they interact with your Westie, they can give him the treats, reinforcing a positive experience.

Other great places to socialize are:
- community days
- downtown shopping areas
- national parks
- puppy kindergarten classes

Bring a supply of treats so that you can pass them out to those who want to say hello to your Westie. When you approach socializing and training this way, it's really not work—it is part of an enjoyable outing. Your Westie will soon think that the world is a really wonderful place, full of interesting smells and treats that appear out of nowhere.

Take note of the things that your Westie seems uncomfortable with— maybe it's grates in the sidewalk, or open umbrellas, or big trucks—and work at desensitizing him to them. Again, treats are an excellent training tool.

Housetraining

If you want to make housetraining successful, stick to a schedule and boundaries. A dog on a schedule

Being Good

How to Give Training Treats

If your Westie is like most dogs, it won't be hard to find a treat that really gets his attention. It could be a hot dog, some soft cheese, dried liver, or something else. Small pieces of treat should be given when you want his full attention. Take the food he adores and cut it up into tiny nibbles so that he can be rewarded frequently and won't waste much time chewing. The idea is to give him a little bit and keep him looking for more. Remember, food is the ultimate motivator for dogs. Remember, too, that training treats count as part of your dog's daily diet.

72

knows what to expect, and this is extremely reassuring for him. A puppy's basic needs (in this department) are to eliminate soon after eating, after waking up from a good sleep or nap, after playing, and of course, first thing in the morning and just before bedtime. If you can be there at these times to bring him to his potty spot, you will be on a fast track to a housetrained Westie.

The truth is, though, that every day is different, and although a schedule sounds like an easy thing to manage, things come up that cause us to deviate from it. However, a couple of missed potty breaks and your Westie will resort to going in the house because he has to go. (To learn more about

Your Westie should want to go into his crate. By gradually introducing him to it, he will adopt it as a second home.

accidents in the home and how to deal with them, see Chapter 7.)

A Crate Can Be Great

As a housetraining tool, some absolutely swear by the crate. Why? Because if a Westie sleeps, eats, and plays there, he will not want to use it as a bathroom. This doesn't mean that if the crate is misused and your Westie is in there for hours on end by himself that he won't have an accident in it. However, if it is a sanctuary for him—a safe environment—he will not want to soil it.

There are all kinds of crates on the market these days: heavy-duty plastic ones that are often suitable for airline travel and can even be folded when not in use; folding wire mesh crates; and even soft-sided ones convenient for transporting your dog. You may want to use different kinds of crates in different parts of your house and even in your car. There are even beautiful wooden crates that can blend in as part of the family room's decor.

Remember, though, that the only way crates will work for you is if your Westie likes being in them. And the way he'll like being in them is if they are safe and comfortable places. This means that he shouldn't be locked into a crate for the entire day, nor should he be left alone without a comfy bed, blanket, toy, and access to fresh water. The crate should not be a prison or holding cell—it should be a private den.

How to Get Your Westie Comfortable With His Crate

To keep the crate from feeling like prison for your dog, you must make it seem pleasant to go in and out of from the very beginning. Outfit the crate with a soft blanket or towel, and put a special toy or treat in it with the door open. While the door is open, let your dog go in

When Accidents Happen

Discovering that your Westie has used your carpet as his toilet is never a pleasant moment. Whether it's because you step in it or suddenly notice the unpleasant smell of a urine-soaked carpet, it's a nasty situation. No matter how upset you are, though, your Westie will not understand your anger unless you actually catch him in the act. If that's the case, shout "No!" and then get him outside as quickly as possible. If you discover the accident any other time, simply clean it up and vow that you will be better about the schedule—and/or will confine him to a more wash-and-wear room, at least while he's still a puppy. Use an enzymatic stain and odor remover specifically for pets to clean up the accident. Doing so will remove the dog's scent and will help prevent him from going there again.

and out of the crate at his leisure. Using treats, encourage him to go in and out by himself. After he's done this a few times, while he's munching on a treat inside the crate, quietly close the door. Praise him for being in the crate, then open the door. Over the next couple days, keep him in the crate with the door closed for longer and longer periods—30 seconds, then 45 seconds, then a minute, etc. If he starts to cry, don't respond in any way and avoid eye contact. He'll eventually quiet down, and this is when you should pop the door open and let him out. You want him to learn that being quiet is his cue to freedom, not crying.

Basic Training

Every well-mannered Westie needs to respond promptly and obediently to five requests: *sit, stay, down, come,* and *heel* (walk nicely on a leash). Everything else is a variation on these essential commands. To be an effective trainer, you must be a leader. Not a drill sergeant, not a friend who will forgive anything—a leader, someone who knows what she wants and can work fairly and consistently for the requested response. If your Westie gets the sense that you're uncomfortable with the training, uncertain about what you want, frustrated, or tense, he will lose focus. Work slowly, practicing these commands by doing them in just a few minutes a day until your Westie responds correctly, and then continuing to reinforce the lessons. As he ages, a well-trained Westie should not need the rigorous trials he went through as

FAMILY-FRIENDLY TIP

Let Your Children Help

The success your child has with training your Westie will depend on how engaged or focused she is. Don't count on a child younger than four to be much help, and with a spunky Westie, a child really needs to be on her game, which may mean that even an eight- or nine-year-old could become discouraged. Be sure that the child follows your lead and does as you demonstrate and request. If your Westie has learned a few things from you, he will likely do the same for your focused child.

a puppy, but a little here and there will help keep him out of the doghouse, as well as tighten the bond between the two of you.

To start all training sessions, your Westie should have on a buckle collar that is neither too loose nor too tight. Attach a 4- to 6-foot (1.2- to 1.8-m) leash to his collar. Arm yourself with a little pouch of soft, yummy, bite-sized training treats. (See sidebar "How to Give Training Treats.") Work in a place where there are few distractions.

Teaching *Sit*

There are so many opportunities to

teach this to your Westie, and you'll find that you ask him to sit so often during a day that it should be something he learns quickly.

Get your Westie's attention by showing him and letting him sniff the tasty treat you have for him. Hold it tightly in one hand, put it near his nose, and while he's attempting to get it, lift it up and toward the back of his head. As he lifts his head to get at the treat, his bottom will naturally go down. When it hits the floor, say "Good sit!" and give him the treat. Repeat two or three times and then take a break. Have another training session just like this a few hours later or when it's his dinner time.

You'll find that there are lots of ways that asking your Westie to sit will fit into your daily routine, such as:

- before you open the door to come back inside your house after a potty break and walk

- before feeding him his meals

- when you return home—and don't pet him until he does!

- when someone comes to visit

- before being allowed out of his crate (or into it)

When your Westie does as you ask, give him a treat and praise him. When he doesn't, simply ignore him for a moment before asking again. With a

Almost all commands work off of the mastering of the sit.

"Sit" Is One Word

Many people fall into the trap of repeating a request if their dog doesn't do it the first time they ask. This is why using food to lure your dog into position and then using the word when he's doing what you want is helpful—it becomes associated with the behavior, not the request. Once the behavior is learned, then the word becomes the trigger for request, not the food. But this happens over time. What you don't want to do is repeat or draw out the word, because this shows your Westie that he doesn't really need to respond the first time. Use your leader voice, body language that conveys you mean business, and be decisive. When your Westie responds correctly, praise him.

tasty treat and a firm hold on the leash to get his attention, he should do what he is told. When he has gone into the *sit* and you're ready to do something else, give him the release word ("okay") so that he knows he can get back to normal, and praise him.

Asking for *Stay*

It's great when your Westie sits or lies down, but how is he supposed to know that you want him to remain in that position unless you teach him *stay*? This is a handy request because it can let your Westie know that you expect him to hold his position for as long as necessary, which can be a few seconds or an extended period. A variation of the *stay* is *wait*, which you can use instead when you only need him to hold still for a little bit.

As with all training, teaching the *stay* should be done gradually, working in short increments over many days. With your Westie on his leash and focused on you, the giver of great treats,

Training teaches your Westie to pay attention to you.

first ask him to sit. When he does, praise him and give him a treat. While he's still in the *sit* position, put your hand in front of his face with your palm toward him, and say in a firm and convincing voice, "Stay." If he holds the position for even a few seconds, give him a treat while you say "Good stay!" Repeat this only a few times, and build the amount of time you keep him in a *stay* very slowly to ensure success.

Asking for *Down*

Going into this one, expect that it will take longer for your Westie to figure out just what it is you want than with the *sit* or *stay*, which are fairly straightforward. Remember that staying down on request demonstrates real trust on the part of your dog. Earn it, don't force it, and be prepared to repeat, repeat, repeat.

To teach *down*, arm yourself first with some tasty treats, as usual. Have your Westie in his collar and on the leash for extra focus and control. Because he's a little guy, sit or kneel down on the floor so that you're on his level but can still comfortably position yourself over him. Often we get on the floor with our dogs when we want to play, and your Westie might misinterpret your action. You want to be able to hold the leash and be above your Westie, yet close enough to him that he can stay focused on what you're asking him to do.

To get started teaching *down*, first ask your Westie to sit. Praise him when he does, but don't give him the treat just yet. Keep ahold of the treat, and

Combining *Sit* and *Stay*

Practicing *sit* and *stay* before meals can be a great enforcement method. The idea is that your Westie will only be served his meal when he can sit and stay to wait for it. When the food is ready, turn to your Westie and ask him to sit. Then use the hand signal with your palm facing his face to ask him to stay. Take a step or so back while he's in the *stay*, then put his bowl on the floor. If he moves without you releasing him, pick up the bowl and start over. Only let him eat when he has stayed for the amount of time you want (not too long, though—he's hungry!). Release him to come for his bowl by saying "Good stay. Okay!"

with his attention on it, begin to lower it toward the floor and slightly in your direction. You want him to have to bring his face down toward the floor and then toward you, which will naturally bring his body into the *down* position. As soon as he is anywhere near a *down* position, say "Good down" and give him the treat. Let him get up, and start over, doing only two or three repetitions for now. Always start from the *sit* position.

Once your Westie gets the hang of it, start asking for the *down* as you are kneeling in front of him. Then start asking for it while standing, incorporating whatever hand signals

It may take a while until your Westie perfects the come *command.*

West Highland White Terriers

you want to use. Always release your Westie with an "Okay!"

Teaching *Come*

Come is an important command. Whether it's wanting your Westie to come in from the yard at night after you've let him out to do his business, or asking him to come to you at the dog park, or even calling him to join you in another room of the house, when you want (or need) your dog to come, you want him to respond instantly—and somewhat enthusiastically. But this is where the Westie's individuality can get the better of both of you. Why should he come to you if you're going to reprimand him? Tell yourself from the get-go that learning this command could take some time, and allow yourself to be pleasantly surprised if your wily fellow responds more

enthusiastically than you anticipated. He may surprise you! Your own enthusiasm can influence the outcome.

Start small and don't expect miracles. This command will take some getting used to on your Westie's part—he would certainly rather be doing something else entirely. Put the collar and leash on, and find a room free of distractions. Arm yourself with those trusted tasty treats. When you're ready, hold the leash and just stand there. This will confuse your puppy to no end, and he will finally figure that he can go investigating on his own. When you see that he's found something else of interest, call his name in a high, excited tone, and say "Come!" while offering the treat. As he moves toward you, make sure that he comes all the way to you to get the treat. Don't repeat the request to come. He must learn that he is expected to come to you when you say it only once. If he doesn't come all the way to your hand, stand back up so that the treat is out of reach, and then take a step or two back and try again. Once he's reached you and gotten the treat, say "Good come," and then "Okay" so that he knows he's off the hook.

Do this a couple times, then take off the leash to end the training session. Remember, ask him to only come short distances, and be enthusiastic in your praise when he is prompt. You'll be able to tell if he's getting it by how well he's responding. After he seems to respond well to the short-distance *come*, train him using a longer leash. Let him get farther away from you before you call him back; practice outside; start calling him to come when you're in another room; and so on, challenging him more and more. You may be tempted to give him a treat for making the effort to come to you, but resist! He needs to come all the way to you before you reward him.

Walking Nicely on Leash

One of a dog's greatest pleasures is being able to get outside and explore. If it were up to them, they'd scamper about going here, there, and everywhere in pursuit of the smell that had their attention at the time. If you live somewhere where you can let your Westie off leash occasionally for a good romp, then by all means do so—it will be really good for him.

However, all dogs should learn to walk nicely on a leash because that is how they're most typically taken out—especially urban dwellers, which many Westies are. It will be unpleasant for you and potentially harmful for your Westie if he's constantly pulling on or tugging at you to go faster or in a direction you don't want to go. This is why he needs to learn to walk nicely on a leash.

Start this process in your home, where you have more control over the environment and the

More Than One Reward

Tasty treats are almost a sure way to get your Westie's attention, but they're not the only way, and you also want to keep him guessing (and working) to please you. Once you see that the treats have served their purpose and gotten him to complete a request and then repeat it, start weaning him off them. If he's reliable, alternate a treat with a pat on the head or an extra-enthusiastic response. If you're working outside, test his training, and if he does what you want, reward him by immediately setting off for a long walk. What you want to continue to do is to associate training with rewards, and these can and should be varied as the training progresses.

SENIOR DOG TIP

Training Your Older Westie

An older Westie, whether rescued or adopted or simply not yet trained, has probably learned some bad habits. You will need to identify those and remind yourself to be patient while trying to help him unlearn them. As for the basics, approach teaching them the same way you would with a puppy: Take it slow and steady, train regularly, and be consistent.

distractions are fewer. When it's time to get the leash on, ask your Westie to sit while you put it on, then say "Okay" to release him as you head for the door. At the door, ask for another *sit* while you open the door—and only open it if he's sitting. It may take a few days before your Westie does this consistently. That's okay, though; it's where you need to start.

After you've gone through the door, ask him to sit again while you lock up. Now it's time to start walking. As you're moving along, randomly ask your Westie to sit for you. If he does, give him a treat and a hearty "Good sit," and immediately start walking again.

If he doesn't, stop walking and stand still. Don't make eye contact, and don't show any emotion.

He may squirm and cry as he wonders what you are doing, but eventually he'll look back at you. Then, ask again for a *sit*. If he's interested in going anywhere, eventually he'll learn that you're in charge of whether and how far he's going to go. If he pulls, simply stop until he doubles back and looks to you for an answer. Ask him to sit, and if he does, reward with moving on.

You'll find in the beginning that your walks are short. That's okay. Slow

If you don't teach your Westie to walk nicely on a leash when he is young, he will run in every direction while on one all the time, possibly tripping you and hurting himself.

progress like down the block is still progress. Reward his effort (and yours) with a more relaxed walk around the rest of the block, stopping to practice every so often if he's getting overexcited and pulling again. Stopping and starting and waiting for your Westie to get it can be extremely frustrating, but keep at it! One day you'll head out, and lo and behold, he'll understand the limits of his leash and will no longer pull. Joy!

The Three Ps

Dog trainers often say that training comes down to the three Ps: patience, practice, and praise. Remember that your Westie will not respond to you if you're grumpy and impatient; he will only become confused. This will set your training back rather than advance

it. If you know that you need to work on something, do it when you can give it your full attention—even if it's just for 15 minutes.

Also, remember that your Westie's perspective on the situation is far different from yours. His way of learning and behaving is also different from that of a Poodle or a Saint Bernard or any other dog you may be tempted to compare him to in your training class. Focus on him and what you want and need him to do, work slowly, and celebrate your accomplishments. You'll be rewarded for your efforts with a bond that is deeper than you ever thought possible. Your Westie will understand you better as you understand him better, and that's what a relationship is all about.

Practice makes perfect, so spend time with your Westie teaching him what you want him to learn.

Chapter 7

In the Doghouse

It's probably clear to you by now that having a Westie in the house isn't all fun and games and snuggling and bonding. You may be spending a lot of time confining your puppy so that he doesn't soil the carpet, or spraying household items with a chew deterrent to keep him from gnawing on them, or running after your little angel as he scampers off with something he's stolen from you.

If you're at your wit's end and you haven't attended training classes in a while, consider calling your dog trainer and re-enrolling. Working with the trainer through some of the problem behaviors your Westie is presenting will help you feel less alone and will lift a huge weight off your shoulders.

Don't be too hard on yourself! Any dog trainer will tell you that everyone, including dog trainers, lets their canine companions get away with things that can be quite naughty. Mostly it's because, to the person living with the dog, the "bad" behavior isn't really that bothersome, or it's mutually enjoyable. An example could be sleeping on the bed with you, even if your Westie is getting territorial about it and becoming angry when you ask him to get off. Things like this, including giving in to feeding extra goodies or permitting excessive barking, are all part of day-to-day dog ownership. Everyone has different limits and expectations, and determining what's acceptable and what's not can come down to how in control of the situation you feel that you are. If you're letting your Westie do something because you can't stop him, that's a problem.

Common Problems

Canine problem behaviors tend to revolve around aggression, barking, begging, chasing, chewing, digging, and house soiling. Westies can be guilty of any or all of these offenses to certain degrees, so let's explore them further.

Aggression

Often, small dogs get away with aggressive behavior because they are easier to stop, or it doesn't seem as if their actions can have really serious consequences. But that's a dangerous, overly permissive way of thinking. If your Westie is territorial and snapping at people or other dogs, he has an aggression problem. It may be a problem you contributed to by overprotecting him, or he may truly feel that he needs to behave this way to protect himself.

Solution

Regardless, don't take it upon yourself to fix this problem—seek a trained professional right away. The longer you put it off, the more serious the

Canine Adolescence

There are some obvious age-related periods in a dog's life: puppyhood, of course, and then the adult years, and then the senior years. But did you ever hear anyone talk about a dog's teenage years? It's true—dogs go through an adolescence of sorts. When they do, they can be as unpredictable as people at that age—not wanting to listen, seeming belligerent, and general naughtiness. For most dogs, adolescence starts around 9 months and lasts until about 18 to 24 months of age. Just be grateful that your Westie can't drive a car!

Exercise can help prevent many problem behaviors from occurring. All exercise, including swimming, should be closely monitored and incorporate several rest periods.

In the Doghouse

problem is going to become and the harder it will be to undo. The last thing you want is for your Westie to be confiscated by the police or taken away because he's bitten someone.

Barking

Westies are extremely sensitive to movement. For centuries, their primary purpose was to detect and destroy critters who tried to sneak past them. When they get excited (by movement, sound, or general activity), they tend to respond by becoming animated, and, well, barking. Although he's not a yappy dog, per se, your Westie's high-pitched barking, if excessive, will quickly drive you, your family, and your neighbors nuts. What to do?

Solution

Dogs who like to bark can be taught to bark on cue, and once they know that you're asking them to bark, you can then teach them to not bark, or "shush," on cue. To teach your Westie to bark on cue, you need to create an instance that will trigger his barking. Ringing the door bell often accomplishes this. As he dashes over and begins woof-woofing, kneel alongside him and sincerely encourage him for a moment, "singing" along with him, and say "Good speak." When you've had enough, stop saying anything. Get up and turn your back to your Westie so that you aren't making eye contact. Wait patiently and don't do or say anything until he stops barking. As soon as he stops, turn around, say "Shush" quite purposely, and give him a treat.

You will need to work on making the clear distinction between when it's okay to bark and what you expect when you say "Shush." This will take time. One thing that definitely won't work is trying to raise your voice over his barking to quiet him down. If you don't like what he's doing, get something he's interested in, like treats, and only interact with him by feeding or praising him when he's doing what you want. Ignore all other behaviors.

Westies who bark in their owners' absence are tough cases. Obviously, if you're not there, how can you work on the behavior? You will probably need to have a trainer come to your home while you're at work. It's a better solution than having your neighbors grow to resent you and your dog.

Begging

Those piercing dark eyes in that adorable face come in handy for Westies, who are well practiced in the art of begging. Westies aren't as obtrusive as larger dogs and will wait patiently by your feet hoping that something will fall for them to pounce on. They'll lie down on your foot to let you know that they're there. They'll look up at you from under the tablecloth. They'll make it seem like they want to say "Aren't I so cute? Don't I deserve a little bit of what you're having?"

The thing about this bad habit is that it typically starts with a completely innocent event, such as a visiting child

giving the dog a piece of her sandwich or other tasty morsel. Your Westie will then think that whenever people stop to eat, he can share the goodies. Any success on his part, no matter how small, will only reinforce this behavior.

Solution

A change of habits is in order. First and foremost, do not offer your dog food from the table—ever. This doesn't mean that you can't give your pal people food; in fact, fresh veggies and steamed meats are very good for him. You will just have to put the leftovers aside and only give them to him in his bowl at his mealtime. The next thing to do is either prevent your Westie from being in the same room with you while you eat, or confine him nearby (in

Your Westie lives for the hunt, so playing fetch with a small ball or animal-shaped toy could help release his excitability.

his crate, for example). He should not be allowed to make eye contact with anyone who's eating. This may be hard for your little furry friend to get used to, and he'll bark and whine in protest. Don't give in! Provide an appropriate chew toy that's lined with peanut butter to distract him if necessary. Over time, your Westie will figure out the rules.

Chasing

Your Westie could become so squirrel-crazy that every time you open the door, he bolts out on a mission to chase down and capture any squirrels in the yard. Or he wants to run alongside cars as they go down the street. Or he pulls you in all directions on walks to try to get to anything that moves.

Solution

One fact you're going to have to accept is that your Westie is a terrier who has been bred for generations to chase and hunt down small animals. This instinct is part of who he is. As such, you may need to make a compromise on your expectations of what he can and can't go after. For example, if he's darting about the yard while you're inside, as long as he's safely fenced in, you may need to just wait while he has his fun. Reward him for coming back inside when you call by having a treat at the ready. If, however, you can't stand your dog's wild ways while walking, extra on-leash practice (as outlined in Chapter 6) may be in order.

Chewing

Whenever your Westie finds and destroys something he's not supposed to, it's upsetting. If it's part of the furniture or a valuable keepsake, it's even more upsetting. For your Westie, however, chewing is fun and engaging. He can't understand at all why you'd be upset.

room will help, too. If he's home alone for a long time, leave a radio or fan on for ambient noise. Owners with busy lives tend to cut back on the exercise they give their dogs, and this is a recipe for disaster—be sure that your Westie is getting enough exercise. Last but not least, consider enrolling him in a doggy day care program for at least one or two days a week if he's by himself a lot. The opportunity to cavort with other dogs is great for him. On the days he's not there, you can hire a dog walker to get him outside.

Digging

This is another trait that is part of a Westie's very being—to get to the vermin he was bred to eliminate, he often needed to dig. Besides serving a purpose, digging can be downright enjoyable for Westies (and many other dogs). So what to do about your eager digger?

Solution

Because Westies love digging so much, you must come to a certain peace with it. There is a way! Instead of punishing your dog for digging all the time, provide an area where he can dig to his heart's content. Designate a space big enough for him to enjoy, and put a box around it so that it's like his own personal dirt- or sandbox. Fill it with loose dirt or sand, and praise him for digging there. If he still digs in spots where you don't want him to, reserve some of his feces and fill the holes with it. When he uncovers his own mess, he should be deterred.

FAMILY-FRIENDLY TIP

A Family Affair

It's important when working on changing any of your Westie's behaviors that the whole family commit to the process. If you want your dog to stop begging at the table, you will have to make sure that none of your other family members give in. This can be difficult, especially if your Westie decides to hone in on the one who's most likely to sneak him a morsel. It may help to remind everyone of what you want to accomplish by posting something on the refrigerator to serve as a reminder.

Solution

Boredom could be a major factor in this problem behavior. The first thing you should do is think about when and where the chewing occurs. Is it while you're not home? Is it only in a particular room, or is it all over your house? Your Westie needs alternatives to whatever objects you don't want him turning into his own personal chew toys. Appropriate, solid chew toys, especially those lined with peanut butter or something enticing, will help keep him occupied and focused. Confining him to a crate or to a single

Hide things (a favorite ball or toy, for example) you know he'll want to dig up in the designated spot to make it more interesting.

House Soiling

Although every dog has an accident occasionally, frequent accidents are a sign that there is either something physically wrong with your Westie or he doesn't understand what you want him to do.

Solution

The first thing you need to assess is the nature of the accidents. Are they mostly urine? Is your Westie pooping in the house? Does he return to the same spot over and over? Does he soil when you're home as well as (or only) when you're not home?

Understanding the circumstances of the misbehavior will help you find a solution. First, be sure that there is nothing physically wrong with your dog. Once you get your veterinarian's clearance for any health issues, go back to the housetraining drawing board (as discussed in Chapter 6). Be diligent about confining your Westie when you're not home (and sometimes even when you're home) and restricting access to the house unless

Young puppies are accident-prone. Be consistent in your housetraining efforts and routine.

If Your Westie Gets Lost

This is something so scary that it's hard to think about, but the fact is that it only takes a minute for your Westie to become lost. You could be opening the front door when the phone rings, turn to answer it, and not close the door properly. An open door is an invitation for a curious Westie, and he could be out of sight in a second. Even with a fenced-in yard, the gate may be left ajar by a neighborhood child, or your little white wonder may dig a hole under the fence. With their curious natures, Westies won't hesitate to go exploring, figuring you'll catch up to them.

The best way to ensure that your dog is returned to you is to attach a good old-fashioned dog tag to his collar. It's the first thing people will look for, and it should have his name and your home and cell phone numbers on it. Another level of protection is the microchip, a rice-sized computer chip that is inserted into the muscle between your Westie's shoulders and can be scanned by shelters and veterinarians should he be turned in at one.

Should your Westie become lost, make a flyer as soon as possible to post in your neighborhood with a clear picture of him on it. Offer a reward. Inform all local veterinarians and animal shelters, as well as your local police and fire departments. Enlist your friends and family to form a search party. Don't give up!

you're with him. Also, reexamine your schedule. Are you taking him out as frequently as you should be? Thoroughly cleaning an area that's been soiled is important, too; use an enzymatic stain and odor remover. Think about what happens when you're out with your Westie and he's supposed to be doing his business. Do you praise him when he goes outside so that he understands that's what you want? Do you walk him only until he goes, then hustle him back inside? If you're doing this, he will soon learn to take longer and longer before he goes so that he gets his walking time in.

A house soiling problem is a serious and complicated one, and if it is truly driving you crazy, you should seek the assistance and advice of a professional dog trainer.

SENIOR DOG TIP

Problem Behaviors With an Older Dog

Your aging Westie is like an aging grandparent—things just start to go wrong, and there's not much you can do about it. Dogs don't complain and can't point things out the way people can, either, so it's really up to you to notice what might be bothering your dog and try to help him.

Some of the ailments of older dogs can be frustrating, especially house soiling, which is common. Be patient with your friend, and try to remember that he is not doing it deliberately; it's just what's happening to his body. Learn as much as you can about the aging experience for dogs, work with your veterinarian, and treasure your Westie's golden years.

All the hard work it takes to properly raise a puppy is well worth it.

Chapter 8

Stepping Out

Westies are one of the true dogs about town. When they're walking the streets, decked out in a matching collar and leash, their eyes sparkling and well-kept fur framing their face, there is nothing that is at the same time cuter or more sophisticated. And the Westie knows that he commands attention as he prances down the street.

Stepping out for you and your Westie involves everything from the daily routine of exercise and doing his business, to strutting his stuff on city streets or the kids' soccer games. Wherever you go, remember to be mindful of others. As your Westie's owner, it is your obligation to indulge him in as many walks a day in as many places possible. Ideally, this could be everywhere you go, and fortunately, the Westie's small size makes this doable.

Common Courtesy

It is the rare terrier who is content to meet and greet without incident anyone who wants to say hello. As a defender of hearth and home, a terrier is always a bit suspicious and always a bit ready to show who's in charge. However, terriers do have large hearts!

As mentioned in Chapter 6, because he is naturally suspicious, the best thing for a Westie is to be exposed to as many kind people and animals as possible as early as possible. Knowing that people will coo and want to pet him whenever they see your Westie, it's especially important that he accept the solicitations of strangers. However, as his caretaker, it's important for you to have your antenna up a bit when you are approached by strangers and strange dogs. A Westie's sense of self-importance, as well as the terrier instinct to stick with it, can combine for an unpleasant scene should an unsuspecting but rambunctious puppy

SENIOR DOG TIP

Traveling With Your Senior

You may think that leaving your pal home is better for him as he becomes slower and stiffer with age, and of course each trip has its own considerations. But don't count him out just because he may be down. A change of scenery can be just the thing to lift his spirits and rejuvenate him—and lead to a good night's sleep later.

Be considerate, though, and don't overdo it. If you used to be able to complete the 5-mile (8-km) loop with him at a favorite park but you haven't done it in a while, don't assume that he'll be fine with it this time. Start with a shorter distance and see how it goes. The last thing you want is to overdo things.

If you're taking a long car ride, your senior Westie may have to relieve himself more frequently or drink more often. Don't forget his medications and his food. And remember, enjoy your time together!

or an overly assertive dog come upon him too suddenly. Be mindful of who and what is around your Westie.

Children will always want to pet your Westie, so carry some spare treats and instruct them in how to offer them. What could be better than a Westie who thinks that every child he sees is going to give him a goody?

Planes, Trains, and Automobiles

The wonderful thing about Westies is that they are small enough to transport easily but big enough that you don't have to carry them in your arms all the time (leaving more room for packages and luggage!). Look around for a carrier that, like your personal luggage, has an extending handle and wheels and is specially designed to transport small dogs. These carriers are made of the same kind of tough material as a suitcase, so they're durable. Once your Westie learns that the carrier is his ticket to ride, he'll soon be asking to get in and join you on your journeys.

Going by Car

This is certainly the most frequent form of travel for all of us and will be for your Westie, too. You might as well go ahead and designate a certain spot in your car for your four-footed travel companion to call his own, because he's going to need one.

The spot you assign (or he chooses) should be one in which he will be safe and secure. You could put your pal in a crate to take him here and there—it's a good idea to do so for traveling long distances—but for the usual trips to the

Before you travel with your Westie, make sure that he is well trained and well socialized.

Family Road Trip!

You and your family have decided to go on vacation and bring along your Westie. You are all very excited. While planning for the trip and thinking of everything you'll need to pack, it is often easy to overlook what your Westie will require. He can't pack for himself, so he depends on you to bring his necessary supplies. If you won't be somewhere where you can purchase the kind of food you normally give him, bring along enough of it to last him through the trip. Bring some water from home as well, and keep it in a cooler so that it doesn't get hot. Extra towels and blankets are a good idea, and don't go anywhere without making sure that your Westie's collar and leash won't break for any reason. A halter can provide a safe and secure alternative to a collar—your Westie can't squirm or pull out of it should he become frightened and make a mad dash for it, and it allows for a bit more freedom and flexibility when he's walking around. Designate a duffle bag or tote for your Westie's supplies so that he has a suitcase of his own in which to store his things.

store or to school or the post office, he will most enjoy being able to look around and take in the sights. You may need to install a special elevated and contoured doggy seat that straps into the seat belt. To keep him from dashing about the car while you're driving, keep his leash on and secure it in a slipknot on the handle beside the passenger door unless he's otherwise secured.

You will need to make adjustments for him and for yourself until the two of you have everything just so. Besides your Westie, his collar (with ID tag), and a leash, there are some other items you should stow in your car so that you have them when you travel together. These include an old towel, whether for making his spot more comfortable or for cleaning up as required; a collapsible water bowl (these are easy to store); a jug of water from your tap and a way to keep it cool on hot days; a first-aid kit that includes whatever medications he might need, as well as your veterinarian's phone number; and of course, waste removal bags (preferably biodegradable ones). Put these supplies in a decorative box in your trunk or backseat, and you'll never have to worry about not being prepared.

With their happy-go-lucky and I'm-part-of-the-action personalities, Westies will want to look out the windows of the car. But putting the window down too far is a bad

Where to Stay

Many lodgings are pet friendly these days, and because you have a small dog, it can be even easier to secure a room. Don't think, however, that your Westie will be welcome with you anywhere just because he's cute and compact. Always do your research, and make your reservations ahead of time. The last thing you need is the aggravation of trying to find something for the two of you at the last minute when it's late and you're tired.

There are several online pet travel sites, but one of the best is www. petswelcome.com, which features thousands of listings of all kinds, from bed-and-breakfasts to ski resorts to campgrounds. Different establishments have different terms for pets who stay, so be sure that you understand all the rules before making your reservation.

The reason establishments have rules is that pets can be unpredictable. You may understand that your Westie barks loudly when it's mealtime and then doesn't bark the rest of the day, but if that time happens to be when the other guests of the hotel are trying to sleep, they will not find your dog's excitement amusing. In fact, they may decide not to stay at that place the next time—so the owners may decide that it's not worth it for them to accept pets. Your Westie is your responsibility while you're on the road, and the two of you should be ambassadors for the breed and for dogdom and always set a great example.

idea. What if he leaned over too far and fell, or saw something he wanted to run after and fell, or jumped out of the car? He may love the feel of the wind on his face, but for his safety, keep his exposure limited. Also, dogs who put their heads out the window risk getting debris in their eyes, noses, or mouths, as well as being accidentally launched from the vehicle.

Riding by Rail

Getting away from the big city by train? No need to leave your Westie behind! There are some passenger trains that allow dogs. Be sure to call the one you're thinking about traveling on, and ask about its regulations. If he's allowed, pack him into his handy carrier, and away you go. The rhythm of the rails will probably lull him to sleep!

Taking to the Air

Airlines are so much smarter about putting dogs on planes now. Almost all carriers have detailed instructions for how a Westie should be crated before he'll be allowed on an airplane. No one wants anything to happen to any animal who is on a plane with them, and the airline personnel feel the same way. Most carrier agents will be happy to help you ensure your Westie's safe passage.

If you plan to take your Westie on a plane, you must make arrangements well ahead of time. You'll want to check to see if your Westie will be able to travel in the cabin with you or whether he'll need to travel in cargo (this is a size consideration and sometimes a policy by the individual airline). Be *completely prepared* before arriving at the airport, and once you're there, know what you'll need to do before and after putting your pal on the plane. Call all carriers that fly the route you're interested in, and ask all the questions you can to determine which one has the best pet policy. It's a big deal to put

The West Highland White Terrier is a beautiful breed. Perhaps you have the perfect little stunner to enter into a dog show!

your dog on a plane, so you must feel completely comfortable about it.

Things to Do With Your Westie

You have surely realized by now that your Westie does not want to take life lying down. He will be happiest (and healthiest) if he is able to participate instead of just observe. Fortunately, there are many things you can do with your Westie that will satisfy his needs and get you out and about, too.

The time you spend with your Westie participating in activities is time that will deepen the bond between the two of you. You'll learn a lot about each other as you put in the time and energy that these activities need. You'll have some great experiences and some not-so-great ones—all memories in the making for you and your furry friend.

Without further ado, here are some of the worlds that await you.

Agility

For whatever reasons, dogs seem to really enjoy participating in agility—it's the fastest-growing dog sport in the country and has been for years. It involves maneuvering a dog through a series of assorted obstacles, from jumps to platforms to weave poles to tunnels, and getting through the course as quickly as possible. Dogs who have the fastest times and the least amount of points against them are the winners. Dogs of all shapes and sizes participate in agility, and it is as thrilling to watch others go through the course as it is when it is finally your turn. One of the most rewarding parts of it, though, is seeing how much fun it can be

FAMILY-FRIENDLY TIP

Junior Showmanship

It may well happen that you and your child (and spouse) may all be bitten by the show bug. While you're competing in regular classes at shows licensed by the American Kennel Club (AKC), your child can get started in the AKC's Junior Showmanship program. Designed for children ages 9 to 18, it's an arena in which juniors compete in a real class in front of a judge. The classes are determined by the number of wins the junior has, and kids can show any breed. It's a great way for them to learn about dogs and dog shows, of course, but also to develop the handling skills they'll need should they continue in the sport.

for your Westie. If you want a fast-paced and exciting sport to become involved in, check this one out.

Canine Good Citizen® (CGC) Program

A CGC dog is one who has passed a fairly simple test that requires steadfastness of temperament in the face of different life situations, such as walking quietly on lead, not being overly afraid of people, being able to hold

Westies are active little hunters, so any sport you can enter where they have to work is a good thing.

a *sit*, and so on. A Westie who earns a CGC certificate from the American Kennel Club (AKC)—the overseer of the program—is one who can truly represent the very finest qualities of the noble West Highland White Terrier. Check out the program through the AKC's website, www.akc.org.

Conformation (Dog Shows)

If you've ever wondered what it takes to end up in the ring at the Westminster Kennel Club show in New York City, you should take a crack at showing your dog. The dogs and handlers who are in the ring at Westminster are real professionals who work very hard to make what they're doing look easy. As with any other highly competitive event, it takes dedication and work, work, work.

You needn't aspire to showing under the bright lights of the big city to enjoy the world of dog shows, though. In essence, a dog show is about presenting your dog to a judge for her opinion of how he compares to the standard for the breed. People who enjoy dog shows enjoy learning absolutely everything there is to know about their breed and then showing off their dog. It's an addicting pastime, as there is always more to learn and always more dogs to compete against.

To see if this world might be right for you and your Westie, find some shows in your area and just go as an observer. See what people do there and especially how people with Westies prepare and present their dogs. Does it seem challenging and fun to you? You may be bitten by the show bug, but you'll only know if you go!

Earthdog Events

For those whose Westies live to hunt or dig, participating in earthdog events will be a dream come true. These events include competitive and noncompetitive trials that help gauge terriers' (and Dachshunds') natural hunting and working abilities. At earthdog events, terriers are first let loose at the opening of a tunnel dug into the ground. They must enter and burrow through it to make their way to a "quarry" that is safely secured in a cage at the end of the tunnel. They will also have to follow a scent trail to find a rodent or other small animal. If you want to learn more, contact a local Westie club to find out if any of its members participate in earthdog events.

Obedience Trials

If you like working with your Westie to teach him various maneuvers, you may enjoy competitive obedience. This sport is essentially basic training taken to the next level—and then progressive levels of difficulty. The way to find out if this is for you (and your Westie) is to start with a basic training class. Because you'll have to master *sit, stay, down*, and *heel* in this kind of class, you'll soon learn whether you have what it takes to inspire your Westie to do what you ask and to enjoy it. Competitive obedience demands precision and accuracy as you perform requested exercises with your Westie. Your trainer can help you achieve this, and over time, you'll be amazed at the teamwork you and your Westie develop. If you think that this is for you, don't be discouraged by others' comments about terriers being stubborn or inattentive in the obedience ring. Find others who have succeeded in the sport who can help keep you motivated.

Tracking

With their exceptional sense of smell and instinct to hunt with their nose, Westies are natural trackers. Remember, in their early days in the Scottish

Active sports will give your Westie the exercise and mental stimulation he craves. They will also help to strengthen the bond between you and your dog.

Highlands, Westies needed to use all their senses, but especially their noses, to locate and extract vermin. The training you'll do in tracking—teaching your Westie to really use his nose and trust his instincts—will awaken the great Scot that he is, and you'll see a transformed friend as he works the course to find the scented glove at the end (which is what tracking dogs are trained to search for).

Your Little Angel at Work

As said before, your Westie will be the center of attention everywhere because he is just so darned cute and irresistible. If you enjoy seeing people's eyes light up when they spot your little friend, imagine how you'll feel when those eyes are the tired, sad eyes of an elderly person, someone recovering from an illness, or a sick child. If your Westie just loves people and you feel that he has the temperament to be a therapy dog, by all means look into getting involved in this. It can be so rewarding, and you'll find that your Westie will know what to do for each and every one of his "patients."

Therapy dogs are evaluated and do receive training (and you will, too), so when the time comes to interact with

Few things in this world equal some quality time with a friendly, loving dog.

people in the therapy environment, you'll be ready. The organizations that oversee this kind of work include the Delta Society, Therapy Dogs International, Inc. (TDI), and Therapy Dogs Inc. This is a great way to share your Westie's love with those who really need it the most.

Resources

Associations and Organizations

Breed Clubs

American Kennel Club (AKC)
5580 Centerview Drive
Raleigh, NC 27606
Telephone: (919) 233-9767
Fax: (919) 233-3627
E-mail: info@akc.org
www.akc.org

Canadian Kennel Club (CKC)
89 Skyway Avenue, Suite 100
Etobicoke, Ontario M9W 6R4
Telephone: (416) 675-5511
Fax: (416) 675-6506
E-mail: information@ckc.ca
www.ckc.ca

Federation Cynologique Internationale (FCI)
Secretariat General de la FCI
Place Albert 1er, 13
B – 6530 Thuin
Belqique
www.fci.be

The Kennel Club
1 Clarges Street
London
W1J 8AB
Telephone: 0870 606 6750
Fax: 0207 518 1058
www.the-kennel-club.org.uk

United Kennel Club (UKC)
100 E. Kilgore Road
Kalamazoo, MI 49002-5584
Telephone: (269) 343-9020
Fax: (269) 343-7037
E-mail: pbickell@ukcdogs.com
www.ukcdogs.com

Pet Sitters

National Association of Professional Pet Sitters
15000 Commerce Parkway, Suite C
Mt. Laurel, New Jersey 08054
Telephone: (856) 439-0324
Fax: (856) 439-0525
E-mail: napps@ahint.com
www.petsitters.org

Pet Sitters International
201 East King Street
King, NC 27021-9161
Telephone: (336) 983-9222
Fax: (336) 983-5266
E-mail: info@petsit.com
www.petsit.com

Rescue Organizations and Animal Welfare Groups

American Humane Association (AHA)
63 Inverness Drive East
Englewood, CO 80112
Telephone: (303) 792-9900
Fax: 792-5333
www.americanhumane.org

American Society for the Prevention of Cruelty to Animals (ASPCA)
424 E. 92nd Street
New York, NY 10128-6804
Telephone: (212) 876-7700
www.aspca.org

Royal Society for the Prevention of Cruelty to Animals (RSPCA)
Telephone: 0870 3335 999
Fax: 0870 7530 284
www.rspca.org.uk

The Humane Society of the United States (HSUS)
2100 L Street, NW
Washington DC 20037
Telephone: (202) 452-1100
www.hsus.org

Sports

Canine Freestyle Federation, Inc.
Secretary: Brandy Clymire
E-Mail: secretary@canine-freestyle.org
www.canine-freestyle.org
International Agility Link (IAL)
Global Administrator: Steve Drinkwater
E-mail: yunde@powerup.au
www.agilityclick.com/~ial

North American Dog Agility Council
11522 South Hwy 3
Cataldo, ID 83810
www.nadac.com
North American Flyball Association
www.flyball.org
1400 West Devon Avenue #512
Chicago, IL 6066
800-318-6312

United States Dog Agility Association
P.O. Box 850955
Richardson, TX 75085-0955
Telephone: (972) 487-2200
www.usdaa.com

World Canine Freestyle Organization
P.O. Box 350122
Brooklyn, NY 11235-2525
Telephone: (718) 332-8336
www.worldcaninefreestyle.org

Therapy

Delta Society
875 124th Ave NE, Suite 101
Bellevue, WA 98005
Telephone: (425) 226-7357
Fax: (425) 235-1076
E-mail: info@deltasociety.org
www.deltasociety.org

Therapy Dogs Incorporated
PO Box 5868
Cheyenne, WY 82003
Telephone: (877) 843-7364
E-mail: therdog@sisna.com
www.therapydogs.com

Therapy Dogs International (TDI)
88 Bartley Road
Flanders, NJ 07836
Telephone: (973) 252-9800
Fax: (973) 252-7171
E-mail: tdi@gti.net
www.tdi-dog.org

Training

Association of Pet Dog Trainers (APDT)
150 Executive Center Drive
Box 35
Greenville, SC 29615
Telephone: (800) PET-DOGS
Fax: (864) 331-0767
E-mail: information@apdt.com
www.apdt.com

National Association of
Dog Obedience Instructors
(NADOI)
PMB 369
729 Grapevine Hwy.
Hurst, TX 76054-2085
www.nadoi.org

**Veterinary and Health
Resources**
Academy of Veterinary
Homeopathy (AVH)
P.O. Box 9280
Wilmington, DE 19809
Telephone: (866) 652-1590
Fax: (866) 652-1590
E-mail: office@TheAVH.org
www.theavh.org

**American Academy of
Veterinary Acupuncture
(AAVA)**
100 Roscommon Drive, Suite 320
Middletown, CT 06457
Telephone: (860) 635-6300
Fax: (860) 635-6400
E-mail: office@aava.org
www.aava.org

**American Animal Hospital
Association (AAHA)**
P.O. Box 150899
Denver, CO 80215-0899
Telephone: (303) 986-2800
Fax: (303) 986-1700
E-mail: info@aahanet.org
www.aahanet.org/index.cfm

**American College of
Veterinary Internal Medicine
(ACVIM)**
1997 Wadsworth Blvd., Suite A
Lakewood, CO 80214-5293
Telephone: (800) 245-9081
Fax: (303) 231-0880
Email: ACVIM@ACVIM.org
www.acvim.org

**American College of
Veterinary Ophthalmologists
(ACVO)**
P.O. Box 1311
Meridian, Idaho 83860
Telephone: (208) 466-7624
Fax: (208) 466-7693
E-mail: office@acvo.com
www.acvo.com

**American Holistic Veterinary
Medical Association (AHVMA)**
2218 Old Emmorton Road
Bel Air, MD 21015
Telephone: (410) 569-0795
Fax: (410) 569-2346
E-mail: office@ahvma.org
www.ahvma.org

**American Veterinary Medical
Association (AVMA)**
1931 North Meacham Road –
Suite 100
Schaumburg, IL 60173
Telephone: (847) 925-8070
Fax: (847) 925-1329
E-mail: avmainfo@avma.org
www.avma.org

**ASPCA Animal Poison Control
Center**
1717 South Philo Road, Suite 36
Urbana, IL 61802
Telephone: (888) 426-4435
www.aspca.org
British Veterinary Association
(BVA)
7 Mansfield Street
London
W1G 9NQ
Telephone: 020 7636 6541
Fax: 020 7436 2970
E-mail: bvahq@bva.co.uk
www.bva.co.uk

**Canine Eye Registration
Foundation (CERF)**
VMDB/CERF
1248 Lynn Hall
625 Harrison St.
Purdue University
West Lafayette, IN 47907-2026
Telephone: (765) 494-8179
E-mail: CERF@vmbd.org
www.vmdb.org

**Orthopedic Foundation for
Animals (OFA)**
2300 NE Nifong Blvd
Columbus, Missouri 65201-3856
Telephone: (573) 442-0418
Fax: (573) 875-5073
Email: ofa@offa.org
www.offa.org

Publications
Books
Anderson, Teoti. *The Super
Simple Guide to Housetraining.*
TFH Publications, Inc.

Arnel, Jill. *The West Highland
White Terrier.* TFH Publications,
Inc.

Morgan, Diane. *Good
Dogkeeping.* TFH Publications,
Inc.

Magazines
AKC *Family Dog*
American Kennel Club
260 Madison Avenue
New York, NY 10016
Telephone: (800) 490-5675
E-mail: familydog@akc.org
www.akc.org/pubs/familydog

AKC *Gazette*
American Kennel Club
260 Madison Avenue
New York, NY 10016
Telephone: (800) 533-7323
E-mail: gazette@akc.org
www.akc.org/pubs/gazette

Dog Fancy
Subscription Department
P.O. Box 53264
Boulder, CO 80322-3264
Telephone: (800) 365-4421
E-mail: barkback@dogfancy.com
www.dogfancy.com

Dogs Monthly
Ascot House
High Street, Ascot,
Berkshire SL5 7JG
United Kingdom
Telephone: 0870 730 8433
Fax: 0870 730 8431
E-mail: admin@rtc-associates.
freeserve.co.uk
www.corsini.co.uk/dogsmonthly

Websites
www.nylabone.com
www.tfh.com

Index

Note: **Boldfaced** numbers indicate illustrations.

West Highland White Terriers

Index

About the Author

Dominique De Vito has been involved in pet publishing for more than ten years. A member of the Association of Pet Dog Trainers (APDT) and the Dog Writers Association of America (DWAA), she is currently a freelance editor and writer who lives with her husband, two dogs, and twin boys on their winery in Ghent, New York.

Photo Credits